Light and Darkness

"Scripture taken from the New King James Version. Copyright ©
1982 by Thomas Nelson, Inc.

ISBN:978-1-950252-08-4

Light and Darkness

By Summer McClellan

Other Books by Summer McClellan

The Impossible Marriage

What Can I Do for God?

Satan Has No Power Over You

Faith, What is It?

Jesus is our Example

Passing the Tests of Life

Dedicated to *Lonna Leigh*

Table of Contents

"I am the Light of the world. Whoever follows Me will never walk in darkness but will have the light of life."

Jesus

{John 8:12}

Preface

I woke up and it was so dark and so black I was terrified. I wondered if I was in hell. I felt something evil was about to overtake me and devour me. My heart pounded heavily, and I gasped for breath. I got up and started reaching for something familiar. I was disoriented and could not figure out where I was. I reached and reached and finally I felt the wall. I felt trapped in a prison. There was nothing but wall. My hands searched the cold wall for something familiar, a door or something. Then I felt it, the light switch. Quickly I flipped it up, and instantly there was light. Immediately I felt relief. I was in my own familiar bedroom. I wasn't in hell and there were no monsters ready to devour me. The light instantly brought me comfort and dissolved my fears. It gave me clarity and brought my mind back to reality. I was no longer blind; I now knew where I was, and I was safe. There was color again not just inky blackness. The light restored me to order. My nightmare was over.

Everything evil and sinister was in that darkness, but as soon as I flipped that switch, the light came immediately and changed things in an instant. Since the time I was a child, I was terrified of the dark, it multiplied my many fears.

This has also happened to me in my life. I went

from darkness to light. It only took an instance. The Light of the world came to me and released me from the darkness. I love Light!

There are two forces and two kingdoms on the earth, darkness and light. Both are present here. While we are here, we can enter into one or the other. This book is about these two opposing forces, light and darkness.

Chapter One

Out of the Darkness and Into the Light

I went from extreme darkness to light in one instant. It was the single most important instant in my entire life. It has been forty years now, since that instant, and yet it still brings tears to my eyes every time I think about it. Only someone who has embraced darkness in the past can know, as I know, the extreme change it is to go from deep darkness to incredible light.

I believe the reason I embraced darkness so deeply is because I was so empty on the inside. It felt so much better than the deep hunger I had at first. I embraced the same rebellion that the kids in the "in crowd", in the area I was living in were involved in. It was like an epidemic.

Smoking, drinking, drugs, sex, and the occult, anything evil, the young people were doing it. Satan had ensnared the majority of us in deep darkness.

My parents tried everything to straighten me out, but it was futile. I was wrapped in chains of darkness and descending deeper into hell. Soon my life became hell. Sin was no longer fun. I had sunk too deep to find my way out and I no longer wanted to live.

What people don't realize until it is too late is that serving the devil brings us to a miserable end. There is nothing at the end of that road but hopelessness and eternal torment. Satan and his cohorts are viler and more hideous than we can possibly imagine. They delight in our torment and will turn on us with a fiendish and hideous delight.

I once read a book written by a man who had formerly been a devout atheist. He did not believe in God at all. What changed his mind about God was he came to realize, through horrible circumstances in his life, that the devil was real. He was working for a company and the owner of the company was an extremely evil man. At a business meeting for the executives, this man raped a fourteen-year-old girl and offered her to his partners for their pleasure. Although not a godly man this atheist was so sickened by the evil he saw displayed on this young girl, he realized the devil was real. His horror at the depths of evil turned him to God. He realized if Satan were real than God was real and turned his life over to the opposite of the evil that sickened him so. The darkness drove him to the light of Christ.

Darkness is so horrible. I went from reveling in darkness to being tormented by it. Satan had me and he was ready to destroy me totally. I was so miserable. I was destroying my brain with inhalants and drugs. I despised myself and Satan despised me also. I became fearful when alone. Strange things began happening. I would hear knocking and doors would open and close. Objects would disappear and reappear. I was tormented, fearful, depressed and miserable.

It was at this point in my life Jesus came to me literally. He walked through the door of my sister's bedroom, where I was lying on the floor, miserable. He stood over me and spoke to me, "Summer, I don't care what you've done," He said, "I love you."

I sat up and hollered, "I want God!"

The darkness inside me was instantly gone and I was filled with light, peace and joy.

Just writing this has me crying. It is my holiest moment. I will never get over what Jesus has done for me.

I recently watched a video online; it was the testimony of a man named John Ramirez. John's father was deeply in the occult and from an early age John was dedicated to darkness. It was all he knew. John became a very high-ranking Satanist. For twenty-five years he served the devil faithfully. He had moved up in the ranks of evil to the point he would actually talk to Satan face to face, and he would carry out Satan's evil orders. He actually called the devil, daddy.

Eventually, Satan turned on John, as Satan does, and John found himself in hell, standing before the devil.

The devil told him he was going to keep him there and John's body would die. As Satan lunged for John to destroy him, the cross of Christ appeared there in hell, in John's hand. Satan was powerless before this cross, he fell back.

John took the opportunity and ran and was looking for a way out of hell when Satan appeared before him again, but the cross appeared again, and saved him again. Then John returned to his body. He immediately gave himself to Christ. He threw every bit of his satanic paraphernalia out of his house; he said he wanted nothing more to do with darkness ever.

The part I loved about watching this video is the emotion that comes over John as he tells how Jesus saved him from darkness. The tears come to his eyes and his voice chokes with emotion. The moment is so holy to him he can barely tell it but watching him is beautiful. It is beautiful to see the expression on his face and hear in his voice the gratitude he feels.

I know how he feels. I felt the same way. Nothing can compare to the moment, when we come out of the darkness and into the light.

It is funny I never thought of it before, but after forty years I asked my sister who was sitting on her bed at the time Jesus came and spoke to me, if she heard the Lord or saw Him when He came through her door. She said no, but she felt His presence so strong in the room she was gasping, it was overwhelming her.

A couple of days after my moment of transformation, I was walking through the house singing. I was happy now, and I felt like singing. I didn't even know all the words to the song I was singing, just a few lines. It was a song from the movie, Oliver.

It went, "Consider yourself at home, consider yourself part of the family, we've taken to you so strong, it's clear were, going to get along."

As I sang, I heard another voice speak to me. It wasn't Jesus, this time it was the Father. Even though I had never heard His voice before that I can remember, I believe I knew it somehow. We come from Him. It was a deep voice, a loving voice, a powerful voice. He said, "Consider yourself part of My family."

I quickly ran to the bedroom and knelt down to pray. As soon as I closed my eyes I was in another place. I was with lots of people, rows and rows of them, and we were all standing around a bright light singing. Everything was brightness, and I belonged with them. I was no longer part of the darkness; I belonged to the light now. Light, glorious light! I belonged to God's family. I was home.

Chapter Two

Three Kinds of Light

This is the message which we have heard from Him and declare to you, that God is light and in Him is no darkness at all. 1 John 1:5

In this chapter we are going to talk about three different kinds of light. They are number one, God's light, the eternal light that comes from Him; this is the first and original light. The second light is the electromagnetic energy called light which God created on day one of creation. And the third light is the sun and stars which God created on day four of creation. One of these lights is spiritual and eternal and uncreated and the other two were created and are physical.

God's Light

We are told that God is light. God's light is an eternal uncreated light that has always existed and always will. This light also exudes power, immense power. God's light has no darkness at all, and God's light will never dim. His light is holy and pure and eternal. It is powerful and mighty.

Light is part of who God is. His appearance is light. James 1:17 calls God, the Father of lights. This is a light that is powerful beyond words and many times brighter than the sun. The Bible describes God's light in 1Peter6:16 as unapproachable. *Who alone has immortality, dwelling in unapproachable light, whom no man has seen or can see.*

I want to give you several firsthand descriptions of the light from God, from several testimonies of people who have visited the Throne of God. The first will be from Jesse Duplantis's wonderful book, *Heaven, Close Encounters of the God Kind.*

First Jesse describes getting weaker as he gets nearer to the Throne of God. When the light from God's throne hit Jesse, he could no longer stand. God's light is so strong those who aren't used to fall. It feels like a massive dose of radiation, but of course it is not toxic. As he is on the floor an angel brings him some fruit to strengthen him, but he remains on the floor. Jesse was lying on the floor before the throne. He would try to lift his head and look up at God, but he couldn't look up for very long because of the blinding light and glory. Jesse describes what he saw.

Although I couldn't look up for very long at a time, I looked up from the floor in the direction of the overwhelming Light, and I saw Him! I saw Elohim, Jehovah God, Yahweh sitting on the Throne! But I saw His feet—only His feet. The Light was so bright that came from Him I couldn't see His face. Now I know why the Scripture says we can't see Jehovah's face and live—at least, I know I couldn't! I had to keep looking down, the Light was so intense. But I looked again, and I saw His hand resting on the arm of the throne. He is so big—you can't describe Him in a dimension. His hand is huge! His body, the form of it, is sort of like energy, spirit. There is a wall around the throne, but the Throne is higher than the wall—that's why you can see the Throne from every direction, from a distance. And that power, that energy-like smoke of God, covers all around the chair of the Throne itself.

I heard a sound, *Whooooooosh!* There was a massive amount of energy in that place. That's the only way I can explain it. It was God's power! You hear that noise, then the energy goes back into Him. There is smoke and power and noise—the place is noisy! And angels are hollering.

Jesse's description of God's throne is my favorite description that I have ever read of it. He describes it so well I can almost see it. He describes it as exciting, noisy and full of glory. Many times, after reading this I picture myself there, like Jesse, lying on that beautiful marble floor. I am trying to lift my head, but the light is too bright, and its power weakens me. So, I lay there listening as I hear huge angels with loud voices giving glory to God, causing the floor to tremble. Smoke is filling the room. The room is so vast that there are countless millions of beings worshipping God. And I am one of them. I belong there. I so look forward to that day!

Light and power are the words Jesse uses to describe seeing God and a massive amount of energy. Jesse is struggling just to look at what is going on around him.

Another account we will look at also describes the throne similarly. It even also describes the feeling of getting weak. This description is from Dr. Rogelio Mills out of his book *While Out of My Body I saw God, Heaven and the Living Dead.* The first thing Rogelio says is,

As I stood before the Throne, the light was brilliant, and I felt weaker and weaker in my spirit body.

A little later he says,

Then somehow, my eyes seemed to adjust to the brilliant illumination! In a way it was like walking in a dark room when your eyes slowly adjust so you can see in the darkness, only in this case it was unfathomable light that my spirit eyes were adjusting to. As my eyes adjusted, I was able to see the outline or form of the Great Almighty God. Seated there upon the Throne, His very image was similar to that of a man, although I could not make out His facial features. The entire congregation was bathed in the most brilliant light that was emanating from the Throne and the One who sat on it. Though this light was predominately white, within it were beams of

multi- colored iridescent light, which reminded me very much of a rainbow or a prism.

This next quick little description comes from Seneca Sodi, who lived over a hundred years ago. This book is called *Paradise, the Holy City and the Glory of the Throne*. This man also describes the Light and power of God on His Throne.

Beyond all my power of description are the splendors of the Throne itself. As we approached nearer the entrance of the great city and to the region of the Father's throne, mighty waves of light and glory came constantly rolling over us, and with them came such refreshing baths of love, peace and joy, that our gladness was indescribable, having reached a degree of perfection never known before.

I saw many who, on account of the majesty, glory and light, were so overcome, that it reminded much of the experience of many on earth during great revival seasons, whose spiritual perceptions were greater than their nervous powers to endure, hence there followed prostrations, trances, faintings, shoutings and kindred experiences.

Seneca Sodi also saw people falling as this light and glory that emanates from God hits them. Seneca also describes the light as coming in waves and filling him with love, peace and joy. God is the source of all light and all power and the closer we get to His Throne the stronger the light and power becomes. And although all our witnesses are in absolute awe of this scene, they all are overcome by the intensity of it. Let's look at one more person's experience. This one was seen by Dean Braxton and described in his book, *In Heaven! Experiencing the Throne of God.*

There is no end to God the Father. He is bright like Jesus with many colors coming off Him. Jesus and God, the Father light up everything. They do not let any darkness in heaven. None at all! Every being there has God the Father and Jesus inside them. They live outside every being and inside every being. They are the light within every living being and creature. Darkness has nowhere to hide.

Dean mentioned that Jesus is also bright. He carries the same light. This is the kind of light Jesus was speaking about when he declared, "I am the light of the world." Jesus has the same quality of light as the Father. Hebrews 1:3 compares Jesus with the Father, *who being the brightness of His glory and the express image of His person.* Of course, we all know, when Jesus was living on earth, He did not appear in all His glory as described by these. Jesus came to earth in absolute humility, not as the King of the Universe but as a servant.

God's light is very real. Even though we don't see it with our physical eyes it is a very real substance, and it is always present. Created physical light is patterned after God's uncreated eternal light, just as earth resembles heaven, but heaven is much more glorious; God's light is far above physical light, and physical light is amazing stuff. It has been baffling scientists for centuries. Let's talk about physical light.

Electro-magnetic Energy, Light

Then God said, "Let there be light"; and there was light. And God saw the light that it was good; Genesis 1:3

The second light, that we will talk about is the light God created on day one of Genesis record of creation. How could God create light, which read about in Genesis 1, when light already existed? Because God created a different light, a physical light, which is the form of energy we call electromagnetic waves. Light is actually electromagnetic radiation that travels in different wave lengths. The portion of electromagnetic waves that are visible to the human eye is a very small portion. Most of these electromagnetic waves are invisible; they range from as tiny as an atom to larger than our planet.

We also know that light travels very fast. The speed of light in a vacuum is 186,000 miles per second. That is extremely fast! Scientists have found out some amazing things about the speed of light, stuff that is hard to understand. Such as a spaceship could leave earth traveling at the speed of light and return to earth several days later and many years would have gone by on earth. I can't explain that one, but the speed of light is very fast and there are all kinds of mysteries there. But as fast as the speed of light is, which travels millions of miles in a minute, God's light is faster, His light travels at the speed of thought. His light travels billions of miles in a Nano second.

Scientists are finding out some very interesting

things about matter and energy and light waves. Quantum physics says that as you go deeper and deeper into the workings of an atom there is nothing there, just energy waves. Those energy waves can be measured, and their effects seen but they are not a material reality, they are electricity. Science now embraces the idea that the universe is made of energy.

God created this source of energy on day one, when he said, "Let there be light." This is the energy that He created all matter from.

As I said most of this energy is invisible, only a small portion of the light spectrum is detectable to the human eye as light. The rest is invisible, but we use it every day. Radio waves carry information, they carry sound to our radios and television pictures are carried to us on invisible light rays.

Einstein's theory E=mc 2 has to do with light, and the speed of light, and mass and energy. This stuff gets really hard for me to understand but it fascinates me. I will try to explain in simple terms what I think it means. {I am going out on a limb here}

Mass which is made out of energy, electromagnetic waves, and energy are interchangeable. So, everything you see such as a table which feels solid is actually made out of atoms which are made out of energy. So, everything is moving, even though it looks solid and the amount of energy it takes to make up something is quite a bit. The amount of energy in something is measured by its mass and volume times the speed of light squared.

{How can anyone in their right mind not believe in

God???!!!! The intelligence in creation is beyond belief! And we that do believe in God, can we even comprehend the magnitude of power and intelligence, plan and intricate design with which are universe is made? It boggles the human brain!!! How could anyone think all this stuff just happened? The intelligence of the design in our universe is beyond our mental capacities to comprehend. On a very tiny scale it would be like finding the most intelligent piece of equipment that mankind has ever designed and saying that somehow over the last zillion years this thing has just formed itself. God is bigger than we can imagine, in every aspect, in size, in power, in ability and in intelligence!}

The next light God created was the sun moon and stars.

The Sun, Moon and Stars

Then God said, "Let there be lights in the firmament of the heavens to divide the day from the night; and let them be for signs and seasons, and for days and years; and let them be for lights in the firmament of the heavens to give light on the earth" and it was so. Then God made two great lights: the greater light to rule the day and the lesser light to rule the night. He made the stars also. God set them in the firmament of the heavens to give light on the earth, and to rule over the day and over the night, and to divide light from darkness. And God saw that it was good. So, the evening and the morning were the fourth day.

Genesis 1:14-19

The third type of light God created was on the fourth day of creation when God created the sun, moon and the stars. The sun is essential to our life on earth.

I will list some of the things that the sun does for the earth.

1. The sun gives us light.

2. The sun keeps the earth warm. Our atmosphere causes a greenhouse effect which keeps the energy in.

3. The sun causes plants to grow. Energy from the sun is stored in plants in a form called carbohydrates.

We eat stored energy, from the sun, in plants that become energy for our bodies. The sun's energy becomes our energy.

4. The sun is essential to the water cycle; water is evaporated and then it rains, watering the earth and giving us fresh water.

5. The earth's rotations around the sun give us our days and nights and our seasons and years.

We have covered three kinds of light all which are from God. Let's talk a little more about light, and the many facets of light in the Bible.

What Else is Called Light

In the Bible we find the word light referring to many things let's look at what the Bible calls light.

Jesus is called Light.

John 8:12 Then Jesus spoke to them again, saying, "I am the light of the world. He who follows me shall not walk in darkness but have the light of life."

Believers are called light.

Matthew 5:14-16" You are the light of the world. A city that is set on a hill cannot be hidden. Nor do they light a lamp and put it under a basket, but on a lampstand, and it gives light to all who are in the house. Let your light so shine before men, that they may see your good works and glorify your Father in heaven."

Light is a kingdom.

Colossians 1:12 and giving joyful thanks to the Father, who has qualified you to share in the inheritance of His holy people in the kingdom of light. NIV

Truth is light, and we are going to lump three together also **righteousness and goodness.**

Ephesians 5:8-9 for you were formerly darkness, but now you are light in the Lord, walk as children of the Light, for the fruit of Light consists in all goodness and righteousness and truth.

God's word is light. *Thy word is a lamp unto my feet and a light unto my path. Psalms 119:105* {Not only is God's written word light, His spoken word is light, it created light}

Deeds and thoughts, are light.

John 3:21 But he who does the truth comes to the light, that his deeds may be clearly seen, that they have been done in God.

Light is exposure.

Ephesians 5:13 But all things that are exposed are made manifest by the light for whatever makes manifest is light.

Light is substance.

Psalms 104:2 Who cover Yourself with light as with a garment.

Light is Essential

Physical light makes it possible for our bodies to survive on earth. The sun makes the earth inhabitable and provides the earth with energy and is necessary for many aspects of our life, food, water, energy and light.

The spiritual light is even more necessary. Jesus' light has come into the world and set us free from darkness. Now we have become children of light, belonging to a kingdom of light. We no longer work the deeds of darkness, but our thoughts and actions should be full of light. This is not a nice little picture the Bible uses, this is a reality, an actual substance, power and energy. We are to no longer walk in darkness, a void, but in light. We should become brighter and brighter as we follow Jesus the light of the world!

Chapter Three

Darkness

Because the darkness is passing away, and the true light is already shining. 1John2:8b

For something to have speed it has to have mass, and light has speed. Light is a substance. Darkness is not a substance. Darkness is the absence of light. Darkness does not have mass and it does not have speed. Darkness only advances at the rate light decreases. Darkness is a void of light.

There is also a spiritual darkness. The properties of spiritual darkness mirror the physical darkness just as spiritual light and physical light are related. This spiritual darkness is also the absence of light, spiritual light or the absence of God.

The kingdom of darkness came into being when Satan fell. He lives in an evil kingdom made of antimatter, dark stuff. There was a time in my life {I talk about in my book *Satan has No Power Over You*} when I frequently saw demons. They appeared to be made out of shadows. They were formed out of darkness and slightly see through and would disappear like a shadow. They were in the form of rats, spiders and other ugly things and would often hide in dark objects.

One time when my husband and I were living near Flint, Michigan, a high murder area. We had been fighting all day. I felt like it was going to get dangerous, things were of control. I took the kids and left the house. Later we came home and went to bed. That night I woke up and there was a huge rat made out of darkness standing in the room. The Lord told me, "It's the spirit of murder." I rebuked that thing in Jesus' name, and it disappeared between the bed and the wall, and we had no more problems with fighting. {For a while}

There is an actual kingdom set up in the second heaven where Satan and his crew operate from. Satan made the choice to operate apart from God, to make a kingdom unto himself. To remove God is to remove everything that is good. It is to remove all life, light, love, goodness and truth. Which leaves us with death, darkness, hate, evil and deception. It is not a pretty picture. God doesn't like darkness He tolerates none of it in heaven, not even a shadow.

In short darkness is spiritual and physical. Darkness is the absence of light. Light is many times stronger than darkness. And darkness has no creative qualities of its own, it is void, it has no color, no creativity.

Darkness and Light are Both Present on Earth

Both light and darkness are present right now on earth. Both kingdoms are present here. Although we have both light and darkness in our world, on earth, right now, in the world to come, in eternity, all light and darkness will eternally be separated. And to those who have already left our world they have already entered an eternity of light or an eternity of darkness depending on which they chose while living on earth, light or darkness.

Darkness gives me a bad feeling. I can sense darkness and I can sense light. I sense darkness from some objects, it radiates off them. Sometimes certain toys or books or objects, they almost seem like they have evil eyes that are looking out at you. One of the darkest things is pornography. The evil radiates from it; I think a demon comes with every issue. There are even some clothes that radiate darkness, and I can't go to most movies because I sense the darkness so strongly. Most movies are inspired by Satan. Thank goodness Christian movies are now coming on the scene. There are places that radiate darkness. I feel it when I drive past them, such as bars and casinos and even some stores. There are even whole areas that seem to have a dark cloud hovering over them.

Light is here too. You get a whole different feeling when you walk into a Bible bookstore than when you walk into a porn shop. And of course, good churches radiate light. I remember when we used to go to a huge church in Florida. As soon as I would walk through the doors, I could feel the light from the sanctuary just drawing me. The feeling was beautiful. My heart would race, and I could not get through the doors to the sanctuary fast enough. That church was so full of light that the whole area around it seemed light.

This is true also in people's homes. I am a home health aide and at each person's home I visit there is a different feeling, like levels of light. Some people's homes seem to be filled with light, and in them I always see Bibles sitting on the table. Others are dark and some seem neither dark nor light, just kind of void.

Both kingdoms, light and darkness are present here, but this is a temporary situation. The time is coming when darkness and light will be eternally separated.

Light is Stronger than Darkness

All of us, before we became Christians, were in darkness, {this is a result from the fall of Adam talked about in the book of Genesis} although the darkness with some is more evident than with others because some are in much deeper bondage than others.

Although darkness seems to be very powerful, it is not as powerful as light. Light dispels darkness. Just as light dispels darkness in the physical realm, it also dispels darkness in the spiritual realm.

My daughter Joy told me about how God taught her about light being stronger than darkness. When Joy was eighteen years old, she had been a Christian her entire life and had not experienced much sin. Someone very close to her told her about his sinful past in detail. The gross darkness he described to her sickened her and oppressed her mind. She did not want anything to do with this person anymore; she felt utter disgust for him. The images of evil were tormenting her, and she became depressed.

The Lord then spoke to Joy, "The kingdom of light is much greater than the kingdom of darkness," He explained. "If you focus on the kingdom of light the kingdom of darkness will disappear."

As the Lord spoke to Joy a picture of a dark and sinister castle appeared in her mind. As she watched a beautiful castle of light descended right over the dark castle and it totally disappeared, it just dissipated. This was a work done in Joy's heart. She said that no longer did the evil things her friend had told her have any effect on her, the torment was gone. If she thought of them, it no longer disturbed her, and she was able to continue her friendship.

We know that light is stronger than darkness. Darkness only exists because light is not present. We can't chase light from a room by turning on darkness. No, it is just the opposite, light always dispels the darkness. In fact, darkness flees the presence of light, both physically and spiritually. Light is greater. We always need to focus on the light.

Darkness has No Qualities of Its Own

Darkness is void. There is no color in darkness, and no creativity or life in darkness. This gives us a little insight into Satan and his kingdom. Satan has no creativity of his own he is a copycat. We know that Satan doesn't create anything, he only perverts what God has created. His only creativity is to take from what is God's and make his own evil, empty version of it. Anything you see in the kingdom of darkness is copied from the Kingdom of Light.

A perfect example is sex. God created sex. He created in the garden between Adam and Eve. In the original form God created sex was and still is something beautiful and blessed; one man and one woman coming together in marriage, in covenant, for a lifetime. And God created certain body parts for sex also; this is also not to be perverted even in marriage. Satan has perverted sex in every way shape and form he possibly can, not just in our age but in every age. He has introduced every kind of perversion possible. I will list some,

fornication, sex outside of marriage

adultery, sex with someone other than your spouse

homosexuality, sex between two people of the same sex

bestiality, sex with animals

pedophilia, sex with children

Sex with fallen angels, which produce Nephilim, evil creatures

sodomy, oral or anal sex

All of these and more are perversions of something God has created to be beautiful.{ You will notice there are many perversions but only one correct way, and that is in marriage.}

Sex the way God created it is blessed by Him. It is full of light and covered with His blessing and brings good to the husband and wife. Perverted sex inspired by Satan is uncovered by light and attracts darkness and bondage to those who practice it and is destructive to the whole man spirit soul and body. Darkness is a counterfeiter.

Sex is only one area Satan perverts; the list is endless. How about religions? If I were to list every religion I would run out of paper. There is only one way to God and that is the way He made for you to get to Him. But there are many false ways, as many as there are religions. The only true way to God is through faith in the blood of Jesus. Satan has multiple counterfeits which only lead to more bondage and more darkness.

Everything in Satan's realm is a counterfeit and a perversion to something beautiful that God has made.

He has perverted, music, speech, even food, anything and everything he can twist and make it harmful and full of darkness he will. Even Satan's last hurrah, the Anti- Christ, will only be a perverted copy of the real Christ. Satan doesn't think up anything new.

Our goal is always the original, our goal is light. Darkness is not the true, but the false. Darkness is void; it is only the absence of light. It has no creativity or color. It is not fullness but emptiness. Our goal is to put away evil and darkness, to embrace the light, our goal is God.

Chapter Four

Chaos to Order

I have always believed that there is a mystery between the first and the second verse of the Bible. *In the beginning, God created the heavens and the earth.* That is verse one, now we move to verse two. *The earth was without form, and void; and darkness was on the face of the deep. And the Spirit of God was hovering over the face of the waters.*

We are told that in the beginning God created earth and now we are told it is a mess. It is dark, it is void and it is completely covered with water. Verse three begins by telling us what God did with this mess. We are not told how the earth became dark and void and covered with water, which is the mystery. It could have been a global flood like Noah's. I am not even going to pretend to know how the earth got in such a mess, because I don't, but I have heard some different ideas. One is that the earth was home to peaceful dinosaurs that ate plants and that Satan injected evil into the world causing them to eat each other, and God subsequently caused an ice age. Another theory was that there were humans that fell, and God flooded the earth as with Noah but there were no survivors. At this time, we are not given this information, we can only guess. Let's move on.

Now for verse three, *Then God said, "Let there be light;" and there was light. And God saw the light that it was good; and God divided the light from the darkness. God called the light Day and the darkness He called Night. So, the evening and the morning were the first day.*

Notice the Bible says evening before morning. The Hebrew word here for evening is the word erev which come from the root word for chaos. The Hebrew word here for morning is boqer which comes from the root word for order. We see that every morning of creation brings order to chaos, evening. And each day of creation God brought order to the chaos the planet earth was in. It was no longer formless and void and in darkness. God repaired the earth to Eden, a beautiful paradise on earth.

This is the characteristic of darkness, or Satan or sin, or evil, it brings chaos to the earth and to our nations and to our homes and our families and to each of us. But when we come to Jesus, to the Light, He restores order to chaos every time.

Light Brings Order to Chaos

I have seen this in my life repeatedly, the light of God bringing order to my chaos. My husband, Jim and I were two completely dysfunctional people when we married. My husband came from a violent past and was also an alcoholic and drug addict. A psychiatrist told him one time that he was trouble looking for a place to happen. It was true.

Then I was sort of just the opposite, I was full of fear and had never developed a personality. I was easily devastated and would cower in fear. This would set my husband off because he took it as rejection. We had chaos! Now add three children who are raised by two dysfunctional adults.

Our house even looked like a war zone, there were holes in every wall and the doors were often broken down.

We were trying to live a normal life, but we were just too broken.

When our home would erupt into fighting and chaos, I would cry out to God, sometimes on a daily basis. In the midst of chaos, His peace would descend. Over and over, He came through for me.

Sometimes I would just be so angry at my husband for drinking. I thought if he would just quit everything would be okay and we could be happy. He would promise to quit, but the promises never lasted very long, and I sometimes was filled with rage.

But God's love and light also dissipated the rage

and anger. Time and time again he restored order to my heart and my emotions. I wrote more about this in my book *The Impossible Marriage.*

God has thousands of times comforted me and dried my tears.

God has rescued us, countless times, from harm and danger, and kept my husband from a life behind bars.

God has rescued my children, from disasters, from rebellion, from evil, and protected them over and over.

He has kept my family from homelessness and poverty, from divorce and from premature death.

He has given us hope, over and over. He has fulfilled our desires and made the deepest longings of our hearts come true.

God has truly made order from our chaos!   But I kept calling on Him and calling on Him. And each time that I did, His light came and dispelled our darkness.

A Young Girl in Chaos Commits Suicide

I saw a testimony of a beautiful girl on, *The 700 Club,* one of my favorite Christian television shows. This girl's name was Tamera Laroux. She very briefly told the host of the show, Pat Robertson, how because of her parents' divorce, her life spiraled downward. She blamed herself and she became very depressed and felt extremely rejected. At the age of fifteen she decided her life would never be happy and she became determined to kill herself.

I listened on the edge of my seat. I knew firsthand

how painful that is; I thought of my own parents' divorce. I never thought I'd get over it. I listened further.

She found her mother's gun and held it to her chest, over her heart. Just before she pulled the trigger, she asked God to forgive her for what she was about to do. Then she pulled the trigger. She died and went to hell. She described in some detail the horrors of hell and realizing she had missed her chance to receive Jesus and spend eternity with Him. The regret she felt was indescribable. As she was in that horrible place the hand of God scooped her up and she was returned to her body. Her thoughts were now of turning her life over to Jesus.

She was raced to the hospital, but God healed her body miraculously and soon she was well enough to go home. Now she had been given a second chance and now she had given her life over to Jesus.

Looking at this beautiful girl now talking to Pat on the show, she was the perfect picture of peace. I wondered if the experience in hell and being saved was the end of her problems.

The host, Pat Robertson asked her the question I wanted to know too, what had happened to her since?

She told Pat that God did not immediately deliver her from the horrible depression that led her to suicide. Her answer surprised me. She said it was a process. She told Pat that she took the promises of God and applied them to her mind and to her emotions on a daily basis.

I gasped.

God in His goodness knew the best way for her. This young girl was not spared from facing this horrible chaos in her mind, which caused her to shoot herself. Instead, God taught her to apply the Word of God daily to her chaos.

I thought of King David's words from Psalms 119:105, *Thy word is a lamp unto my feet and a light unto my path.* Tamara was taught by God to apply light, through the word of God, to her damaged mind and emotions on a daily basis. The results were amazing, this beautiful girl radiated peace and joy as she told her story. She went from chaos to order, from turbulent to peace as a result of God's light being applied to her situation through His word. Light has always and will always bring chaos into order.

God Will Again Restore Order to the Planet Earth

When Jesus returns to earth for the second time, He will restore order. There will be no more wars or chaos. Satan will be bound in the bottomless pit for a thousand years and peace will reign on earth. We read about this in Isaiah 11:6-9

The wolf shall dwell with the lamb, the leopard shall lie down with the young goat, the calf and the young lion and the fatling together; And a little child shall lead them. The cow and the bear shall graze; Their young ones shall lie down together; And the lion shall eat straw like the ox. The nursing child shall put his hand in the viper's den. They shall not hurt nor destroy all my holy mountain. For the earth shall be full of the knowledge of the Lord As the waters cover the sea.

He shall judge between many peoples, and rebuke strong nations afar off; They shall beat their swords into plowshares, and their spears into pruning hooks; Nation shall not lift up sword against nation, neither shall they learn war anymore. Micah 4:3

When Jesus comes to earth, order will be restored, and peace will again reign like in the Garden of Eden. All that is out of order with the earth will be corrected.

This is the result of God's light; He brings chaos to order just as He did in Genesis.

Just as He has done for me, He changed my personal chaos to order. And also, His word brings light and order as Tamara LaRoux found out. Soon God will bring His order permanently, when He permanently casts out darkness, and His Light will continue forever.

Chapter Five

The Light of His Face

And the Lord spoke to Moses, saying: "Speak to Aaron and his sons. Saying, 'This is the way you shall bless the children of Israel. Say to them:
The Lord bless you and keep you;
The Lord make His face shine upon you,
And be gracious to you;
The Lord lift His countenance upon you,
And give you peace," 'Numbers 6:22-27

I love the feeling of sitting in the sunshine. It is a warm peaceful feeling that is so relaxing it will put me to sleep. It is also good for us. The sunshine will give our bodies a boost of vitamin D and it will even kill germs and help us heal. It is beneficial to our bodies and even helps combat depression. We need the sunlight. But the light of the sun pales in comparison with the light of the face of God.

We have already read some first-hand testimonies which attempted to describe to us the indescribable brightness of the face of God. No one seemed to be able to see into the extreme brightness to actually see the face of God. The light of God's face is incredible light. And even though it is further from us than the sun, its power is beyond compare and it travels at a much greater speed, it reaches us in an instant.

This blessing given by God to Moses, blesses us with the light of God's face shining upon us. I love this powerful blessing, it was given to us by God, and it is divinely inspired. We know the darkness will flee from us with the light of God's face directed toward us. The peace from this light is incredible. It quiets and calms our spirit and gives us rest. It is divine energy and power directed at us. It provides life and protection, healing and deliverance. It also gives us a connection to the heavenly realm, a light connection.

God Sends Summer an Angel with a Shining Face

I have often talked in my books about my years of delivering newspapers for a living. Those years were very difficult in one way and wonderful in another. The wonderful part was the angel that went with me every night.

I had delivered papers before, so I knew how dangerous it was. A woman alone often on foot, in the middle of the night, in a high crime area, it was very dangerous. One woman paper carrier had been killed. There had been several drive-by shootings in the area of my paper route.

But our finances were dire, and I had to do this. I prayed as I began my new route, "God I have to do this, I can't do this alone. I am just going to put my protection in your hands and go without fear."

God answered that prayer in such a wonderful way. I immediately felt such peace. The peace was so delicious and warm that I actually enjoyed being out there every night even though I was tired!!!! I didn't get to sleep through a night for over three and a half years. My youngest daughter Joy, who was seven at the time, went on the route with me the most. She also felt the incredible peace.

Soon God showed me the source of the peace. I had a very large angel with me every night. He sat on the roof of my car. He took up the whole top of the car. The interesting thing about my angel companion was his face. It was very bright and shining. My angel would keep his shining face turned toward me at all times. When I would get out of the car and deliver papers to a building on the left, the angel remained on the car but would turn his face to the left. I could literally feel his light shining on my back as I would go off to the left and deliver papers. It felt wonderful. This angel ministered the same way God ministers in this blessing, with the light of his face. I believe it was God ministering to me, I believe the light of God's face was shining on me through this angel.

The Light Connection

The amazing thing that Joy and I found as we would go on the paper route together was that in this angel's presence we could see better in the spiritual realm. We could actually peek into heaven. We would try. Joy could see much more than I, but we would describe to each other what we were seeing, and we were seeing the same thing.

I remember one night in particular. My husband Jim has always loved horses and he used to work at a horse farm. We were wondering if Jim had a horse waiting for him in heaven. We both immediately saw his horse, it was beautiful. We wondered if we could see the barn so we both tried to look. Then we both saw the barn where his horse was kept. I had never seen a barn like it. It was all brick; red brick and it was made in a circle and the stall doors all faced out. It was big and it was the most beautiful barn I had ever seen. Joy described it to me as she was seeing it too.

Often while I was busy delivering papers, Joy would be visiting her room in heaven. Heaven and the spirit realm became very real to Joy. The presence of the angel, and the light of his face, seemed to be our connection.

Just as I learned to feel the presence of my angel

and his light shining on me, I have learned to feel that same feeling when I pray this blessing. I feel the light of my Father's face shining on me, that glorious light. There is more to it than light. It is approval, from our Father. Because of Jesus giving us right standing with the Father, we can experience the Father's blessing. The approval of our Father for us and His blessing on our lives, as we stand in the glorious everlasting light of His wonderful face shining down upon us. It makes things right in our souls.

The Blessing

I just recently read a book called, *The Blessing,* By John Trent PH.D. and Gary Smalley. This book describes the importance of receiving the blessing from our earthly fathers. The author has found in his counseling practice that his patients who did not receive the blessing from their earthly fathers were not able to move on to a healthy life. They were lost and looking for approval. They longed to receive love and approval from their father, but some never did.

The book describes a man named Brian; whose father had his whole life planned. Brian's father had been a career Marine officer, and his lifelong dream was for Brian to follow in his footsteps. No love or kind words were given to Brian as his father was trying to make him tough for the military. When Brian did well at something his father would tell him how he could have done it better.

Brian did join the Marines and his father was

thrilled but it was short lived. Brian did not do well in the military and was dishonorably discharged. Now Brian's father wanted nothing more to do with him and would not even allow him to come to his house.

Brian struggled in his life with feelings of inferiority and lacked confidence. He worked at jobs which were beneath him. And even though he almost married three times, his relationships failed. That's when he came to the author for counseling, who exposed the reason for his failure in life, the lack of his father's blessing.

Brian is not alone; many are struggling through life searching for the approval they never received from their father and unable to receive love because they feel unworthy.

If a blessing, received or not received from our earthly father can have such an affect, how much more healing and powerful is a blessing from our heavenly Father?

Summer Receives Blessing from the Heavenly Father

When I came to the Lord, I had a very damaged self-esteem. I felt I was worthless. God the Father began to work on me. He had a lot of work to do.

My twin sister, Carol and I had been fatherless {except for a horrible stepfather when we were very small} until my mother remarried when I was around seven. At the age of eight our new dad adopted us. Having a dad was a dream come true for us. But as wonderful as it was my dad and I often butted heads. We were total opposites. My dad was motivated, smart, self-disciplined and successful. His plans for my sister and I were that we would go to college and become successful also.

My sister Carol and dad seemed to hit it off fine. She was a straight A student, and she went to college. But I felt like I was a disappointment to my dad. He tried to get me to think and make wise choices. I was not capable of operating like that. I was like a person who had a huge bomb that had gone off on the inside of me. All there was inside was a huge hole. It was a gaping hole where a person should have been. The whole consumed me, and I had no plans for the future, not even thoughts about a future. He was in a world that I could not live in. I did not go to college; it was all I could do to finish High School.

We especially disagreed on my choice of a husband. My husband Jim was on parole from prison when I met him. Jim had never lived successfully out of jail before. None of that mattered to me. I didn't think like that. What mattered to me was that Jim had touched my heart in a way that no one ever had before. In a matter of minutes of being with him he warmed my cold heart, and filled that gaping hole, more than I knew was possible. I was led by that inner need, not by reason or thought or even common sense. I had to be with him every minute of every day and that was my reality. Nothing else mattered.

My dad and I were in two different worlds. Dad's world was realistic and mine wasn't. When Jim asked my dad's permission to marry me, dad didn't say yes, and he didn't say no. I understand that thirty-five years later but at the time it wounded me deeply. It magnified my feelings of worthlessness and I felt like Jim, and I were both worthless.

Then my heavenly Father began to deal with me. The most amazing thing was that He understood me completely. He came into my reality with me. And He began to repair me. The process took many years.

There were many things the Father began to speak to me. I will tell you a few but the process could take a whole book. Each time God brought up an issue in my heart He began to reshape me on the inside. Each time He spoke He gave me His blessing and each time He spoke He changed me a little more.

One time I had just hung up the phone my with my dad. I was married by this time and pregnant. I was hungry because I was out of groceries before payday as always and I had called my dad hoping for a pizza. Things didn't quite go as I hoped. Dad told me I needed to get used to it because Jim wouldn't ever be able to make enough money to live on.

After I hung up the phone, I asked God, "Is that true?"

I heard no answer at first, but the Father began to answer me over a period of several weeks. He started pointing to things and highlighting things that were being said or going on around me and at the end of several weeks He spoke, and like a puzzle He put it all together. One of the things He highlighted was a song we sang at church that Sunday. The words were, **Oh I marvel at the wisdom of our God, when I see the little lily pushing up** the stubborn sod and I marvel at the wisdom of our God, When they crucified the Father's only Son, and they put him in the tomb they thought they'd won. But just like the little lily He rolled back the stubborn stone and I marvel at the wisdom of our God.

There were many little things He kept pointing out and then He put them all together and He spoke. He told me, "Jim has the potential to make more money than most men because of My principle of 'In your weakness you are made strong in MY strength.' Any area in your life that you are weak you can walk in My strength and because Jim or you do not have the ability to make money, if you turn that area to Me, you will have greater ability than most. You have My strength. You both are like the little lily and Jim has great potential."

God took me from hopeless to great hope with His answer. Now Jim and I have never made huge amounts of money, yet, {could happen} but we did increase, we got to the point we didn't run out of food every week, and that was because of God.

My dad was a practical man, and he was just calling it like he saw it. I had made choices that led me to the predicament I was in. But God spoke His blessing over me and opened a door of hope that made a way for me. God's blessing was not earned by me; it did not come because I was good enough or because I had done something to deserve it. No, God spoke this blessing over me simply because I am His child.

He continued to give me His blessing. One time I was praying, and my parents' dining room table kept coming to my mind. I didn't understand why, so I just kept pushing it out of my mind, but it kept coming back. "God, are you bringing this table to my mind?" I asked.

"Yes," I felt He said.

Why would God want to talk about a table? I thought about the table. It was my mom's dream table. My mom had longed for that table and my parents had gotten it together. It was beautiful and expensive. Also, it was the only thing that they fought about during their divorce. For the most part the divorce went easily except for the table.

At this point God interrupted my thoughts. "Why did they fight over the table?"

I thought about it and then answered God. "Because my dad didn't want my mom's new husband to be able to take it. Dad said he wanted Carol to have it someday."

My dad had carefully planned the divorce settlement so my mother's new husband could not easily take her for everything. His calculations were correct. He took her for as much as he could then left.

God continued asking questions. "Why did he want Carol to have it? Why not you?"

God was prying deep into the unsaid. The unsaid in my family was that Summer was the black sheep, the irresponsible, sloppy one. "Because" I answered, saying the unsaid, "I ruin everything and I don't deserve it, Carol should have it."

Pain stabbed through my heart as I said it, but I knew it was true. It was understood. I was not the good daughter. I was the one that kept them pulling out their hair through the years. I did not deserve anything good, and I knew it.

"Yes, you do." God told me, touching a deep wound and healing it, one that I didn't even realize was so deep and so painful until He brought it out. It's kind of funny but years later I ended up with that table.

God, the Father has given me His Blessing, over and over. His light has entered the dark places in My heart, the places of hurt and pain. His love has brought light to those places and His words to me have healed me.

We have the Blessing of God the Father! The light from His face is shining upon us. We have this, through the blood of Jesus and through faith in Him.

Is Your Face Shining?

We have seen in the Bible a few places where, like God, someone's face has literally shone. One such was Moses, when he came down from the mountain, after spending time in the presence of God. His face was so bright they actually put a veil over his face. Another one was in the book of Acts. Stephen, the first martyr, as he was about to be stoned, looked up and saw heaven open and he saw God on the throne and Jesus at His right hand. The Bible tells us Stephen's face shone like an angel.

As we gaze upon the face of the Father, our face will begin to shine too. There is also a light inside us that we need to let shine. It shines through the windows of our souls, our eyes. It is love. It will touch those around us. Remember light is invisible energy that travels very fast in waves.

When you look at others, is the light of your face shining upon them? We are children of God the Father now, we are children of light, as the Father does, we should do also.

Do you look at your children with love and let the light of God shine upon them? Do they see unmerited acceptance and love on your face simply because they are your child? Or are you constantly scowling and showing disapproval?

Believe me I have used the scowl of disapproval with my children. It is the lazy way of correcting them, and I used it. Just scowl for a second, they get the picture, but only if it is rare.

Our children should not see a scowl every time they look at us. They should see the light of our face. They should see love shining from our eyes to them that tells them they are loved unconditionally.

And what about your spoken word? Are you speaking the blessing over your child? Blessings need to be spoken. There should never be any strings attached to the words "I love you." They are loved unconditionally simply because they are your children.

How do you look at your mate? What do they see when they look at your face? Is it shining on them, like God's does on us, or do they have to earn your approval?

Is your face shining God's light to the world? Is it

reflecting the light of God to the others?

I remember when I was a teenager before I became a Christian. I remember going to church and the feeling of disapproval I received from the adults there. They would look at me like I was the worst. {and I was} They certainly did not shine with God's love.

But there was this older lady; she wasn't from church, but she was a Christian. She worked at a cake store around the corner from us. Her name was Pearl. We were the worst bunch of kids ever, but she didn't seem to notice. We would go into the cake store just to talk to her. She always said what nice kids we were. She would talk to us and smile at us. When the phone would ring, she would stop talking with us and take cake orders.

I hated it when the phone rang. It took Pearl's attention away. I loved talking to Pearl. She was old but she was fun. She would teach the girls in the neighborhood to do the Charleston. All this while she was working at the cake store in between taking cake orders. She always seemed to have time for us. She never seemed to think any of us were bad, even though some of the boys were real thugs. She knew all our names and we could always depend on her for a kind word. Some of the boys would steal anything that was not nailed down. I don't how she dealt with that, but she seemed to love everybody. She was a rare adult. I think we thought at the time we had her fooled. I am sure we didn't. She was giving us unconditional love. The kind God gives. She was letting her light shine on us.

God's Chosen Blessing

God's chosen blessing has to do with the light shining from His face.

While I was writing this chapter my daughter, Joy, called me for prayer. She said that David, my grandson, was afraid in his room tonight. That was strange because David has never been afraid of the dark. She put David on the phone, and I asked him, "What is going on, honey? You are not usually afraid of the dark?"

"It is just in my room," he said.

Joy put the phone on speaker so we could all hear and asked me to pray. I wasn't sure how to pray at first, so I just began asking God to protect David, when all of a sudden, I thought of this chapter and praying God's chosen blessing. So, I did. I prayed that God would bless David and keep him and make His face to shine upon him and lift up His countenance upon him and give him peace. I felt peace so we all said, "Amen."

Joy left David's room and continued to talk to me. She had seen into the spirit realm as we were praying. She described it to me, "Mom as you started praying, I heard two demons talking, and they were in David's room. When you started to pray the one said to the other, 'Ah, she's not very sincere, this is nothing.' "Then she told me. "But when you prayed about the light of God's face, light entered the room, and I heard the demon shriek in terror, and they instantly fled."

David hasn't had any trouble since. This reaffirmed to me how powerful this prayer is. It is God's chosen blessing.

God's angels also often minister to us with the light of God shining from their faces. God's face shining upon us is even more beneficial to us than the sunshine. It gives us peace and protection and chases away the darkness. God blesses us with unconditional love, simply because we are His children. And we, as His children, have the ability to shine His love as He does, on our families and on others. The closer we get to God the more we can illuminate His light to others.

For it is the God who commanded light to shine out of darkness, who has shone in our hearts to give the light of the knowledge of the glory of God in the face of Jesus Christ.   *2 Corinthians 4:6*

Chapter Six
The Rainbow

And God said, "This is the sign of the covenant which I make between Me and you, and every living creature that is with you, for perpetual generations: I set My rainbow in the cloud, and it shall be for the sign of the covenant between Me and the earth. It shall be when I bring a cloud over the earth, that the rainbow shall be seen in the cloud; Genesis 9:12-14

Rainbows are made from light. Isaac Newton, in 1666 discovered if he passed white light from the sun through a prism, it would split the light into a band of colors. Each color comes from light with a different wavelength. The band of colors that appear are called the spectrum and they always appear in the order of red, orange, yellow, green, blue, indigo and violet. Basically, rainbows appear from the white light passing through the raindrops like a prism.

The Rainbow After the Flood

After Noah and his family got off the ark, God promised Noah that He would not destroy the earth with a flood again. This is when God told Noah about the rainbow. God said the rainbow is a sign. It is a sign of His covenant.

God had to destroy the earth because of the extreme evil on the earth at that time. The evil was so great that God was sorry He had made men on the earth. That is pretty bad. The earth had become a living nightmare. Fallen angels and women had borne children together which were vile creatures called Nephilim. They had tampered with the human DNA, not only with fallen angels but also with animals. The earth was filled with a tampered mankind, beings inspired by Satan. Because of this, the earth had become filled with violence. The Bible tells us that every intent of man was only evil continually.

There have been times, since Noah's time, when groups of people on earth became so vile that God commanded the Israelites to destroy everyone, men, women, children and even animals. The Nephilim reappeared on the earth again, several times as mankind progressed into evil again and at times and God would send the Israelites to destroy them. This is because humans were mating with fallen spirits and animals again as in the days of Noah and had to be destroyed again but not on a global scale. This was how the whole earth was in the days of Noah, all life, except Noah and his family and the animals God brought to Noah, were destroyed. The Bible tells us the last days also will be this way.

After the flood, God had restored order and Noah, and his family began again. God began this new day of hope, with His rainbow in the sky. The rainbow is a sign of His covenant with Noah, and the generations to come and with every living thing on earth. It is a sign of hope. God has and always will restore order and cut off evil, His will is always good.

The Rainbow Around God's Throne

Another place that a rainbow is seen is around the throne of God. In Ezekiel 1:28, Ezekiel describes the rainbow he sees around the throne, *Like the appearance of a rainbow in a cloud on a rainy day, so was the appearance of the brightness all around it. This was the appearance of the likeness of the glory of the Lord.*

God took the likeness of the rainbow which surrounds His very Throne and put it in the sky as a sign of His covenant.

Remember all of our witnesses to the throne in chapter two; they all also described the rainbow. I will mention Seneca Sodi's here.

Enoch now led us to the throne itself. It was encircled by wonderful, majestic bands of light with all

the colors of the rainbow, which signified the attributes of the Almighty God and Father of us all. We seemed to comprehend God as we never had before. I thought of the band of light that encircles the planet Saturn, the gold tinged clouds of an earthly sunset; but no comparison could describe its glory. Beneath the circle of this rainbow was the seat of the Almighty Father. For beauty, grandeur, glory and majesty, it cannot be described. It was simply upholstered glory, with all the colors of the rainbow tinging everything.

This is the original rainbow, the one that proceeds from the light of the Father, the one that every other one has been patterned from. This rainbow around God's throne is not a decoration to make His throne look pretty. No, it is the radiance of His attributes.

Each of His attributes emits a different wavelength of power and brilliance which emits a frequency and a color. Similar to the color caused by light on earth, but on earth without the divine attribute attached.

Isaiah 11:2 lists the seven Spirits of the Lord and each one has a corresponding color of the rainbow.

The Spirit of the Lord --Red
The Spirit of Wisdom—Orange
The Spirit of Understanding—Yellow
The Counsel of God—Green
The Spirit of Might---Blue
The Spirit of Knowledge—Indigo
The Spirit of Fear of the Lord—Violet

Seven Feasts and Seven Priorities

The colors of the rainbow have even more significance. There are seven colors in the rainbow. God often does things in sevens. There were seven days of creation. There are seven notes in music; these are also related to color. There are seven feasts that God established, which correlate with seven priorities and events that will happen on earth. The first four feasts are already fulfilled, and the last three feasts will be fulfilled. Each color of the seven colors of the rainbow goes together with each of the seven feasts. I will list the seven feasts, priorities and colors that go together.

1. The Passover, God's first priority is the blood of Jesus. **Red.**

2. The Festival of Unleavened Bread, God's second priority is fellowship and communion with God. **Orange.**

3. The Festival of first fruits. Jesus is Alive. **Yellow.**

4. Pentecost, the promise of the Holy Spirit. **Green.**

5. The festival of Trumpets, priority of Go tell the world. **Blue**.

6. The Day of Atonement, Jesus' atonement is everlasting. **Indigo.**

7. The Festival of Tabernacles, The return of Jesus. **Violet.**

Symbolism of Color

The colors of the rainbow also have symbolic meanings. I will list a few,

Red—the blood of Jesus, love, anointing, passion, power

Orange—perseverance, wisdom,

Yellow—glory of God, gift, welcoming, honor

Green—growth, prosperity, nature

Blue—divine revelation, spiritual, heavenly

Indigo—in secret, mysteries, Holy Spirit, truth

Violet—royalty, kingship, luxurious

These are all positive meanings. On the other hand, each of these colors can have a negative meaning. Darkness cannot create color. Satan only imitates, he never creates.

Red—anger
Orange—danger
Yellow—cowardly
Green--envy
Blue—depression
Indigo—cold and uncaring
Violet--false authority

Rainbows are Special

I love seeing rainbows. Every time I see one it is an event. It fills me with a sense of awe. But rainbows have meant even more than that to me. There have been times when they have been a sign to me from God. They were dark times in my life when I needed hope, at these times, I have seen rainbows. And at these times I have received hope believing they were a sign to me from God.

One time was when I was twenty-four years old. I had been married for five years and I had two little ones, one and three years old. My husband, Jim and I had just had a huge miracle happen. My husband was facing a long prison sentence. I need to explain that my husband although he is a Christian has come from a very bad lifestyle. He had actually never lived a normal life, and he drank daily to cope with his pain. He had been incarcerated all of his adult life when I met him and had been in and out of institutions since he was a young teenager. Although he was married to me and had two children, he had not overcome his past and had gotten arrested for felonies three times since we were married five years. This was his third. He was facing a long prison sentence, but God miraculously delivered him. {I wrote more about it in our story, my first book, *The Impossible Marriage.*}

Instead of prison Jim was checking himself into an alcohol rehabilitation facility for three months. I was going to be alone. Jim was not the only one who was dysfunctional. I depended on Jim for everything. He faced the world while I hid. I did not know how I would support myself and the kids or what I would do without him. We had no money. We had moved to a different town the year before to be near my twin sister and at the same time Jim was leaving, my sister moved to a different state. I never felt so alone. I knew God was going to somehow help me through, but still I was afraid, and I didn't know what would happen.

The day before Jim left, we took our two little ones and took a walk to the little park that was in the middle of the small town we now lived in. It was a rainy day. We did not know what was up a head for us, or how I would survive, but God had just come through with such a miracle for us. But still we were only part way. We were trying to figure out what I was to do, but we had no plan. We were virtually penniless. As our little family walked back from the park, we turned around and saw a beautiful rainbow. I knew that I knew that I knew that God was giving me a sign. He was telling me there was hope for my family. It was His covenant, His promise, we were His and He sent me this rainbow to remind me.

I gasped when I saw it. "Look Jim," I said, "God's telling us everything is going to work out for us."

We stood there in awe gazing at the rainbow until it faded. I felt hope renewed. Then as we were almost home the thought hit me. "What if was just a rainbow? What if it just happened and it really wasn't God speaking to me."

I prayed silently to myself, "God, if that was really

You telling me everything is going to be okay. Will you give me another rainbow?"

As I finished my prayer, I looked up at the door of the store we were passing on our walk home. I had passed this store a hundred times on our daily walks to the park, but I had never noticed it before. There was a sticker about eight inches tall above the open sign; it was a picture of a rainbow. My prayer was instantly answered.

I gasped again. God was going to take care of everything, and this time I laughed out loud. "How does God do this stuff?" I asked myself.

God did provide. The year before, when we had moved, here our little mobile home we owned had never sold. We would have had to let it go because we couldn't pay the lot rent on it, but my mother needed a place to stay and moved into it. In my mind I had let it go. I never expected to receive a penny from it. But it sold and I received enough money to live on until Jim was able to come home and resume taking care of us. I even had enough money to buy some things I had needed.

The rainbow gave me hope; it lifted me up when I was apprehensive about the future.

More Rainbows from God

There were several other times too. The most dramatic was when I was working at an assisted living home. One of my patients was dying. She was a woman only in her sixties that had Alzheimer's disease.

For several days I had been keeping a vigil at her bedside with her daughter. Her death lingered on for many days and we were both very tired. Finally, the end came. Her mother drew her last breath. We had been sitting there for days waiting and now it was here, and it felt so draining. I don't know what I expected, a light or something but it was just anticlimactic. It felt so tragic.

This daughter who had a young daughter of her own sitting by her mother's bedside for days. She had really lost her mother years before because of her disease. Her mother had not known her or spoken to her for several years, and now she was gone. It was such a dark moment for both of us. I was feeling the daughter's pain and emptiness. There was no sign of the person her mother had once been and now she was gone.

All of a sudden life and death seemed so gray. I had to get alone and cry, the depression was choking me. Her daughter felt the same way; she stumbled from the room her mother was in and into the main room.

Suddenly, I heard her cry out, but it was not a cry of sorrow, it was a cry of joy! I ran into the main room where she was. That whole end of the home was windows, and we were high on a hill overlooking all of the Grand Traverse area where we live. Her daughter had looked out the window and there was the most beautiful double rainbow. It was more than a rainbow! It was heaven opening up to receive her mother. It was hope! It changed the atmosphere from dismal to pure joy!

Once again, God brought hope through His sign. The same sign he gave Noah, the rainbow.

Rainbows!!! God's sign to us of His love and His covenant. He will always be there for us to restore order, give us hope for our future and make a way when it looks like the end.

Rainbows are a sign given to all of us. God has not deserted His plan for the earth. He is here present with us. He will put an end to all that is wrong because He is our hope. The rainbows we see on earth, as beautiful and awe inspiring as they are, they are only a foretaste of the rainbow that proceeds from God. It is His light that proceeds from His divine attributes that sends off color and frequencies of such immense power and beauty that even in heaven only those who have prepared themselves are strong enough to look upon the majesty of His light and presence.

So next time you see a rainbow, take hope, God is remembering the covenant He has with you, through Jesus, He is giving you a sign. Take courage, look up, it is His sign to you. He has a plan. He will restore order, and all will be well.

Chapter Seven

Clouds

"Behold God is great, and we do not know Him; nor can the number of His years be discovered. For he draws up drops of water, which distill as rain from the mist, which the clouds drop down and pour abundantly on man. Indeed, can anyone understand the spreading of the clouds, the thunder from His canopy?" Job 36:26-29

My daughter, Joy, was telling me what she saw in the spirit. We were driving to the park to let the kids play and ride their bikes. Even though the sky was dark with possible rain and the wind was blowing, it was one of those days when the wind was warm, and it felt good to be out. Joy was telling me her latest spiritual experience while the kids were chattering away in the back of the van. I love to hear about her spiritual experiences. I have always felt like I have a female Moses for a daughter. Her prophetic experiences thrill me. She works a midnight shift and prays all night long while she is working.

"You know what I saw last night mom? It was a

dragon."

"A dragon? Sounds awful."

"Well, I thought it must be an evil dragon, because I thought all dragons were evil. But it wasn't. He told me that he was a servant of the Most High God. You know mom, not all the angels look like humans. God had dragons that fell but not all of them fell. This was a good dragon."

I had never heard of such a thing. I wanted to know more. We let the kids out of the van and off they went running through the park. Joy and I got out too and began to walk the trail; it was my favorite kind of weather. Thrilling weather. A storm was brewing, and the clouds were blowing, and the wind was warm and invigorating. We knew we didn't have much time before the rain came. Joy continued telling me about the dragon.

"Mom, do you know what dragons do?"

I had no idea.

Joy continued. "They mark territory. This dragon was marking our city for the Lord. He was traveling around the perimeter of our city, marking it as God's territory. God is doing something special here, Mom."

This I knew. God had moved us here from Florida some years ago. He had told me He was going to do something unprecedented in our city, which is why He moved me here.

Things like this are so exciting to me. All I could say to Joy was, "How cool!"

A long low cloud passed overhead, and Joy looked up and gasped. "That's him," she hollered. "That's him." I looked up as a dragon shaped cloud passed quickly overhead and another followed similar to the first.

We stood and watched in amazement. The rain started and we began to run toward the car.

After that, I became obsessed with clouds. I could hardly drive all summer long, looking at the clouds. It was not the first time by any means that I had heard of special clouds. I have seen pictures of Jesus face in the clouds. One is a famous picture, this cloud appeared at a T.L Osbourne meeting, in 1956 in Java, it was a sign and a wonder. As T.L. preached in a Muslim nation, Jesus' face appeared in the cloud before the meeting. The picture was so clear that it looked like a painting in the sky. It was beautiful.

Also, in 1994, we went to a large church in Florida that experienced an awesome time of revival. Strange clouds kept appearing over the church. They were seen by many. Some saw horses and some saw a huge hand. Some saw red clouds that looked like fire.

And I know many, many people have seen angels in the clouds. If you want to see some pictures, just google angels in the clouds, they are breath taking. Suddenly I was looking at the sky all the time. I was hooked on clouds.

Joy called me a few weeks later. It was after one of her nights of prayer. "Mom, the Lord told me why we see things in the clouds."

"Why?' I asked.

"Remember what Aunt Carol told us about water?"

"Yes." I replied thinking of the interesting conversation I had with my sister.

My sister, Carol, had been studying about water. It was fascinating, she told Joy and I about it. This is what she learned. A Japanese man named Dr. Masaru Emoto has made some amazing discoveries about water. His discoveries are almost too strange to be real and yet they are real, and many scientists are making similar discoveries.

Dr. Emoto has been freezing water molecules and looking at them under a microscope. He has found some startling things. Water responds to spoken words. When they said the word love, over the water molecules, they formed a beautiful design. It looked like delicate lace. When they said the word gratitude, the molecules formed a different beautiful design, but it was much plainer than the word love. When they said the word hate, the water molecules formed an ugly blob. When they said Adolph Hitler, it was gruesome.

This is only the beginning. They could even write words over the water, and it responded. Also, water molecules looked different when they would take samples from different places. In beautiful places like waterfalls the water molecules were beautiful. In city pipes they looked like little pipes, small little angles.

It got even stranger. They discovered water has a memory. Every person that handles water causes the water molecules to look different. Each individual makes a different imprint on the water molecules! They discovered any substance or outside influence made some sort of an imprint on water. Music made a beautiful imprint. Prayer made a beautiful imprint. Negative words made ugly imprints. They discovered water can record and store information by the way that water molecules join together.

They even made discoveries with water that had been affected positively, by positive influences. Bakers found it made better bread. They tried it in swimming pools and were able to greatly decrease the chlorine and no algae developed. They tried it in a factory and the water needed much less chemicals, saving them money.

Dr. Emoto pointed out the human body is mostly made up of water. The things we say and do can greatly affect our health. Water is amazing stuff!!!!!

{While I was learning this, I thought of my husband getting after me because I always forget to bless my food. According to these studies the water in my food will literally change for the better as a prayer is said over them! I decided to start blessing my food!}

{Okay, let's get back to clouds.}

Joy reminded me of what we learned about water.

"Mom," she said, "Clouds are water. God told me that all these things we see in the clouds are not the angels that we are seeing. They are an imprint in the clouds. Like the water molecules' reacting to what is going on around them, the clouds which are water vapor are doing the same thing. God said the clouds show us, like the water does, what is happening in the spiritual realm."

"Wow!"

Now my eyes were really glued on the clouds. Now Joy and I share cloud stories. When we see demonic forces in the clouds we pray. We see clouds as a window to the spiritual realm.

Joy and her family were driving to the beach at Lake Michigan one summer day. This day she saw a strange cloud, but it was not good. She said it reminded her of a pirate ship. She and her family began to pray and immediately the cloud dissipated. They had prayed and the evil dispersed.

Clouds can be a window to what is happening in the unseen ream. Someday we will see something even more exciting in the clouds. The Bible tells us that.

Then they will see the Son of Man coming in the clouds with great power and glory. Mark 13:26

Chapter Eight

A Tale of Two Cities

There are two kingdoms on the earth, the kingdom of light and darkness. There are also two kingdoms in the spirit realm the same two kingdoms.

But let's first see these two kingdoms in the natural realm, and how they have influenced mankind on the earth. Each belongs to a city.

One is Babylon and one is Jerusalem. It is not so much the city and actual place I am talking about, although that is part of it. It is more than that. I am talking about two opposing forces on the earth that are very real and affect every human being that has ever lived on this planet. We see these kingdoms and their beginnings thousands of years ago, after Noah's flood.

The only people on the ark with Noah were his wife and his three sons and their wives. Noah's son's names were Shem, Ham and Japheth. From them come all the people on earth.

Babylon

Out of these three sons the earth became repopulated. Soon the giants reappeared. They came from Noah's son Ham's descendants. One of Ham's grandsons named Nimrod became a powerful king on the earth. Nimrod was a giant, and he was extremely evil. Nimrod started the great organized worldly apostasy from God, which has been prevalent on the earth from ancient times until now. He formed an organized system against God; this is the system that Satan works through.

Nimrod was born in 1908 B.C. And he ruled for 185 years. He incited the people against God. God had commanded after the flood that the people spread out over the earth.

Nimrod persuaded men not to obey God. Instead of spreading out they gathered together in one place and built a city, that city was Babylon. He set up humanism, an idea that rejected God and depended on their own strength and his. He claimed depending on God was for cowards. He gradually changed the government to tyranny to bring them to a constant dependency on himself. It was Nimrod who incited mankind in the plain of Shinar to erect the tower of Babel.

The tower of Babel was to be an affront to God. According to the historian Josephus, Nimrod had the purpose of avenging himself on God for killing his forefathers! To build a tower tall enough to withstand any flood God might bring again. They made it with burnt brick cemented together with mortar, so as to make it waterproof. It was to reach such heights that it would stand above any flood. As the rebellious, men on earth worked together under the evil control of Nimrod the tower was built quickly and sturdily. This is when God in His ultimate wisdom confused their languages. This dispersed mankind and spread them out into colonies according to the languages.

Nimrod began idol worship, human sacrifices and humanism. The false deities in every culture began with Nimrod. Nimrod's laws decreed that the Babylonians should not look to the God of Noah but should be ruled by human governments, an idea which humanists still hold to today. He is the beginning of the Anti-Christ system which will continue until we see it arise as the beast in Revelation which again will defy God, in this same spirit, and ultimately declare war on God in the Battle of Armageddon.

Nimrod was eventually killed, according to the book of Jashur, by Esau, the grandson of Abraham. Nimrod's evil wife Semi ramus, who was also his mother, propagated after his death, an evil doctrine of the survival of Nimrod as a spirit being. This was the beginning of Baal worship. She claimed a full-grown evergreen tree sprang up overnight from a dead tree stump. Her claim was this was the springing forth of the dead Nimrod to new life. Every year on Nimrod's birthday which was December 25, she claimed Nimrod would visit the evergreen and leave gifts on it. The tree was to be decorated with gold and silver balls, symbolizing Nimrod's testicles. {gross!] Semi ramus then bore a son which she claimed was a reincarnated Nimrod and made herself and her child a mother son deity. She was called the queen of heaven. This deity is still worshipped today although it has been mixed with Christianity and called Mary and Jesus.

Nimrod, inspired by Satan developed an evil kingdom of darkness on earth that operates in complete rebellion against God. Nimrod's ideas are alive and well in the earth today; his birthday is even celebrated as the biggest event of the year. This mind set is the spirit of the world and is totally opposite to the way God's kingdom operates. I did not even realize how much of this mind set I held to, which was totally opposite from God's; I will talk about that later in this chapter.

Babylon is the seat of the anti-God empire on earth. It is the capital city. It is the mecca of the arch enemy of God and His ways. It propagates many lies for men to follow, lies that deny God's word and power, such as evolution. Also, such ideas as following your own heart and not depending on God and pursuing pleasure as the meaning of life. It is set up in defiance to God and it still exists and operates on the earth today. It is Satanic in origin and Satan is behind it. It is the lifting of man in pride and rebellion against God, and millions follow its ideas and ways.

Jerusalem

Shem, the older brother of Ham and son of Noah, chose to follow the Lord. Shem was a godly influence on the earth. Shem was one hundred years old when the flood came, and he lived another five hundred years after the flood. From Shem's grandson, Abraham, God made a people on earth for Himself. Abraham was on earth about the same time as Nimrod. Abraham was born in 1947 B.C. {I find that date very interesting, because that date is very significant to Israel, in 1947 A.D., Israel was being born as a nation.}

Abraham obeyed the command of God, and left the land of Chaldea, in the land of Haran, and dwelt in the land of Canaan.

Now the Lord said to Abram:
"Get out of your country,
From your family
And from your father's house,
To a land that I will show you.
I will make you a great nation;
I will bless you
And make your name great;
And you shall be a blessing.
I will bless those who bless you,
And I will curse those who curse you;
And in you all the families of the earth will be blessed." Genesis 12:1-3

Abraham was 75 years old when he left Haran and

he lived to be 175 years old. Abraham lived in obedience to God. He came out of the land of idolatry and darkness and lived a life of faith and obedience to God. Abraham and his wife Sarah were childless. God promised Abraham a son, which was Isaac, who was born to them when they were past the age to have children. Through this family line, God called out a people for His own, a people who served Him and worshipped Him, a people through whom His laws would come. And a people from whom His salvation for the earth would come.

In Jerusalem, on Mt Moriah, Abraham would prove his level of faith and obedience to God. God called Abraham and told him to sacrifice his son Isaac on an altar on Mt Moriah. As rebellious and full of defiance for God as Nimrod was, Abraham was completely the opposite. Abraham brought his son there in obedience to God to sacrifice him as God commanded. God did not allow him to do it though. God called from heaven and stopped Abraham and then provided a ram caught in a thicket for Abraham to sacrifice.

We have two opposing kingdoms arising after the flood. One is evil, beyond belief, proud arrogant and defiant. And the other one is good, willing to lay down everything precious in utter obedience and faith to God. One is Babylon and one is Jerusalem.

Jerusalem is the capital of the world. It is the place God has chosen for Jesus to reign in the future, as king, on earth. It is the place the temple was built by Solomon and the place where the Jews worshipped. It represents the kingdom of light. It represents a completely different mindset than Babylon.

The kingdom that will never end and the kingdom that will stand is, of course, the kingdom of God. Many years after Abraham's days in the year 605 B.C. Daniel, a young Jewish man was taken into captivity by Nebuchadnezzar, the king of Babylon. Nebuchadnezzar had a terrifying dream, it was a dream about the future of his kingdom, which lasted until the time of the end.

His dream was about a large image, it had a golden head and chest and arms of silver, then its belly and thighs were of bronze, its legs were iron, and its feet were of iron and clay. As the king watched in his dream a stone was cut without hands, which struck the image on its feet of iron and clay and broke them into pieces. The whole image, gold, silver, bronze, iron and clay together and were crushed together and swept away by the wind so that no trace was found.

Kind Nebuchadnezzar could find no one to interpret the dream. He was putting all his wise men to death until Daniel came along and interpreted the dream. Daniel told the king, the large image represented Nebuchadnezzar's kingdom, Babylon, not only then but all the way through history until the end of the age. He told the king the dream was about the future. The rock cut without hands was Jesus and His coming kingdom.

And in the days of these kings the God of heaven will set up a kingdom which will never be destroyed; and the kingdom shall not be left to other people; it shall break into pieces and consume all these kingdoms, and it shall stand forever. Daniel 2:44

God has allowed this evil kingdom to exist for a time, but the time is coming when He will allow it no longer. It will be destroyed and never be seen again.

But God has established a holy line of people on the earth, the children of Abraham, the Jewish people and the Christians, his children through faith. From the Jewish people, the descendants of Abraham we have received the Bible, God's holy Word. From this godly line all the earth has been blessed. From this line Jesus was born.

Jerusalem is the physical manifestation of the kingdom of light. But that doesn't leave us out. We as believers have become sons and daughters of God.

But you have come to Mount Zion and the city of the living God, the heavenly Jerusalem, to an innumerable company of angels, to the general assembly and church of the firstborn who are registered in heaven, to God the judge of all, to the spirits of just men made perfect, to Jesus the Mediator of the new covenant, and to the blood of sprinkling that speaks of better things than that of Abel Hebrews 12:22-24

Summer Worships an Idol

Sometimes God has to weed the idols we worship out of our lives. That is what happened to me. I was inadvertently worshipping an idol. My idol was Christmas. I loved Christmas. I would start shopping in September. I didn't have extra money for gifts so I was always trying to squeeze a little money out of my budget and trying to find some halfway decent thing that was on clearance, so I would have something to give the people on my Christmas list. A few years when my budget was really low, I would make presents. One year I crocheted everyone a pair of slippers. I was crocheting day and night for months.

I always started Christmas early. I would put up my tree on the first of November. I would obsess over Christmas. Mostly trying to get presents with no budget. It would become the most important thing to me for many weeks. I would tell the Lord I would spend more time with Him as soon as His birthday was over. {I had no time for the Lord I was too busy with the hustle and bustle of Christmas}. And when Christmas was over, every year I would get a major attack of the blues. I couldn't understand it but every year I would go through it again.

Every Christmas season I was always looking for a feeling, the Christmas feeling. I was really hooked. It affected my thinking. Every time we would move the first thing I would think of when we came to a new place is where the Christmas tree would go. As the years went by, my Christmas decorations had increased until I had nowhere to put them all. I had no idea I was worshipping an idol, and that the mindset I entered every year was not from the kingdom of light. No wonder it left me reeling every year when it was over.

It all came to an end one day at a prayer meeting. My sister and I and my daughter Joy who was homeschooled, met at the church every Wednesday morning to pray. Sometimes other ladies from the church would join us. It was the highlight of our week. The presence of God was always there and each time we met to pray was new and exciting. Because the meeting was so small, we felt freedom to just let God do what God wanted to do. This particular day God went to work on my idol. He put His giant thumb on me and pressed.

My sister Carol had something that had troubled her for a long time. It was something she didn't understand that had happened a few years before. She had been praying at the church she attended, at that time, with some of her friends. The Spirit of God was really moving on them, and a couple of the ladies began to "run the church". {We are Pentecostals, we whoop and holler and sometimes when the spirit really moves upon us, we run. I love it!} My sister Carol and her friend were running. Carol could sometimes feel very inhibited but this time she just let herself go and was enjoying a freedom in the spirit as she ran the church.

[It is not just getting up and running for you non-Pentecostals. It is like praying in tongues or dancing in the spirit, even us fat ladies can do it, it is energizing, and the Holy Spirit is in it. In fact, I was in a powerful meeting one time when many people began to run, and it was like their feet were so light and so quick that you could barely see them move. I watched in awe as I could hardly believe what I was seeing. They were running and their feet were barely touching the floor. The air was just charged with electricity and those who were running were being called to new things in God.]

As Carol and her friend were running the church her friend fell. She fell and she hurt herself badly. This frightened and confused my sister Carol because she didn't understand how that could happen. It was something she needed to clear up, a trust issue between her and God. How come when she was branching out to something new in God, how come He let that happen?

Because it was just us, {Carol and I and Joy} that week in the prayer meeting, we decided to pray this thing through, it had been bothering Carol for a couple of years. So, we began to pray about it, and we were not going to stop praying until she got an answer.

As we prayed Carol began to remember something. It was Christmas time when this happened, and her friend fell right in front of the Christmas tree as she was running past it. As we prayed, we felt the Lord was focusing on the Christmas tree. I couldn't imagine it, what could possibly be wrong with a Christmas tree? I loved Christmas trees! They are all about the birth of Jesus, right? The more we prayed the more we felt that something was not right about the Christmas tree. That she was attacked by Satan as she ran pass this Christmas tree.

Uh oh, I didn't like this, and I was having a war inside me. This is when I felt this giant thumb begin to press on the inside of me. I was having this giant conflict going on inside of me. If God doesn't like Christmas trees, for some odd reason, that means I would have to give up mine. I don't want to give up my Christmas tree, I love my Christmas tree.

I didn't realize what a hold this thing had on me. I thought I was totally, one hundred percent sold out to Jesus, but I wasn't. I wanted to hang on to my Christmas tree, the idea of giving it up was a real struggle. I wanted to just stop praying and forget this whole thing, but the giant thumb pressed harder. I felt squeezed. I couldn't stop praying and it seemed that there was no one else in the room but me and this giant thumb that was pressing on me, it was God's thumb.

I loved Christmas and Christmas trees and lights and presents. But the question was did I love them more than God? Of course not! Finally, something broke and I had a thought, "Okay, I will get rid of my Christmas tree. I will buy a giant manger scene and we will put our presents around the manger scene."

I couldn't believe the sacrifice I was making but it wasn't enough. The giant thumb pressed even harder.

Suddenly I saw the manger scene in my mind. It was plain and simple. It was the Son of God coming to earth in absolute and utter humility. It was God emptying Himself.

Then I remembered something, it quickly came to my mind. When I was fourteen and newly saved, I went to the Holy land. My sister and I went on a tour with a gospel group. We were taken on the tour to Bethlehem, to the place where it was believed Jesus was born. When we got there, it disgusted me. A Catholic church was on it, and they had completely covered it with gaudy junk. Religious nonsense to me. It was all that overly decorated, holy, holy stuff. I thought, "Yuck! How gaudy! It looks nothing like a manger."

Suddenly the picture in my mind of a manger scene with all our presents around it wrapped in bright paper was equally repulsive and gaudy. The manger was a symbol of humility; I had never seen it this way before. It was a revelation of humility, and the presents didn't belong there. The thumb was pressing harder.

"No presents either God?" I asked.

Now I was thinking of all my Christmas loot. I had a whole box of Christmas videos, and we watched every one every year. I had a singing mailbox that sang about Christmas, a singing radio that reported an unidentified flying object, Santa and his reindeer. I was struggling over each item. I wanted to keep them. The thumb just kept pressing down. I thought of my family they would never understand, and all the people I was supposed to give presents to every year and the list kept getting bigger as our family was getting bigger, babies and more babies, what would I tell them?

Suddenly I didn't care anymore. Even though it was unthinkable to me, I was no longer going to celebrate Christmas. No presents, no tree, no decorations, the war in me was over. I had let go. Life seemed unthinkably boring without Christmas, but I didn't care, no one would understand, but I didn't care. My kids would be disappointed, but I didn't care. I had just given up my idol. The giant thumb released me.

I opened my eyes and finally spoke to my sister. "I don't think I can celebrate Christmas anymore." I said, knowing she was unaware of the giant struggle I just had with God.

Carol said, not completely convinced of that, "Let's do some research on Christmas trees and see what their significance is."

"Okay," I told her but to me it didn't matter. It was a done deal. I was no longer celebrating Christmas.

Strangely enough, after I rid myself of all my Christmas junk and informed everyone in my life, I wasn't doing Christmas, it was like a giant burden was off my shoulders. I was free. I didn't have to come up with stuff I couldn't afford. I never could get people what they really wanted anyway because I shopped clearance sales. And suddenly I had lots of closet space, all that Christmas junk took up all my closets.

Carol researched Christmas and that's when we learned the truth about its origin. It had come from Baal worship. It was Nimrod's birthday. It really wasn't a Christian holiday at first. Its origin was from a false religion. Carol no longer wanted to celebrate either after her research.

But I still had some questions about all this for God. So, I asked Him. "Is it fair to my family not to give them presents? Isn't it a good thing to give presents?"

God communicated something to me, and it wasn't with words. It was spirit to spirit, but I will try to say it with words. He showed me that the spirit of the world, that ungodly kingdom of darkness, is very materialistic. God never meant for us to acquire piles of stuff. But He does want us to have everything we need. And when we no longer need something, He wants us to pass it on to someone who does. This is how His kingdom operates by giving and sharing. He does not want us to be materialistic like the world. He wants us to be givers. I saw that all that

Christmas giving I had done all those years was worthless, to Him and to me, and even to those I gave things to. I gave them something I could find in clearance and hoped it would look like I spent more than I did. It wasn't necessarily what they wanted or needed; it was just junk.

Then He told me the kind of giving He wanted me to do in place of the Christmas giving. He said, "I want you to give people what they need when they need it. Do not give because it is a special day but give when someone has a need. I want you to meet people's needs."

I realized something. The holidays of this world promote the ideas of this world. They promote materialism and greed. They keep our eyes on ourselves and not on God. They are a distraction from what matters. And yes, people give to the poor on holidays, but what about the rest of the year?

God actually did set up holidays that promote our kingdom, the kingdom of light and they are the Jewish feasts. And as with everything God does, they are extremely beautiful and full of meaning. In fact, the Jewish feasts are portals. Heaven is open to us during those times.

I want to say something to you, my readers. My idol was Christmas. It was wrong for me to celebrate Christmas but that does not mean that it is wrong to celebrate Christmas. It was for me because I had made it an idol. I gave up Christmas many years ago, but I still love the story of Jesus birth. I can hardly think of it without crying. It is absolutely beautiful. Yes, I go to Christmas Eve services to celebrate that. I sing beautiful Christmas carols.

I never really got chills about the birth of Christ while I celebrated Christmas; I got my chills from Santa and his sleigh. But now my focus is back on Jesus. Last year on Christmas Eve, I went to a nearby church that I don't usually attend. As I was sitting there, enjoying the service, I felt the most delicious peace, more peace than I had felt in months. It was an absolute feeling of well-being. My daughter Joy who was sitting next to me leaned over and whispered in my ear. Joy often sees angels.

"Mom," she whispered, "There is a huge angel on the stage, and he is handing out little gold presents to anyone who will take them."

Somehow, I knew I had gotten one, because it was a supernatural peace I was feeling. "Can you see what is in the presents?" I asked her.

She concentrated for a moment and then leaned over and said, "It looks like a bubble."

"It's peace." I said.

Joy nodded.

Suddenly I thought of a patient I take care of. I am a home health aide. She is a crippled old lady who lived alone and was often depressed during holidays. I asked the big angel on the stage. "Could you give Martha one of those?"

I wondered if she would receive it because many times she decides to be depressed. I found out two days later when I went to get her up. I didn't tell her about the angel with the presents, she wouldn't understand. But she said to me, "I was watching a Christmas concert on P.B.S. on Christmas Eve, and I got the most wonderful feeling. It just felt like Christmas."

I knew she got her present and had received it. I loved mine too, that peace lingered with me for days. God's presents are the best.

Two Cities

I am so glad I gave up my idol. I wasn't worshipping God. That part of my life was still in the worldly system. There are two kingdoms on this earth, two capital cities, two mind sets. One is darkness and one is light. One began on a plain in Shinar and will end in a plain called Armageddon. It is flashy and loud. Its lights can be blinding. But its light is dark light. It promises you everything but really it gives you nothing. It stands for a life of rebellion against God. It believes that we live apart from God and violently opposes Him. It creates all kinds of theories and ridiculous ideas such as evolution and humanism. It lies and propagates lies. Its king is Satan the father of lies. I used to belong there, but not anymore.

The other city was built on obedience to God. It can look plain. It was built when a man chose to leave everything he knew, so he could obey God, that was Abraham. And the king of this city left His throne in heaven and came to earth in humility and obscurity to lay down His life on a cross. That was Jesus. Those who belong to this city do the same. This city is light, it is true light, the one I belong to, the Light of Christ!

Chapter Nine

Emitting Light or Darkness

As a man thinketh in his heart so he is. Proverbs 23:7

So Jesus said, "Are you also still without understanding? Do you not understand that whatever enters the mouth goes through the stomach and is eliminated? But those things which proceed out of the mouth come from the heart and defile a man. For out of the heart proceed evil thoughts, murders, adulteries, fornication, thefts, false witness, blasphemies. These are the things which defile a man, but to eat with unwashed hands does not defile a man." Matthew15:16-20

In our realm, the physical realm, things like our thoughts and attitudes can be hidden. Someone may conceal their true motives. In the spirit realm this is not possible. Because things like love or hate can be seen. Everything has a frequency and emits energy, including emotions, thoughts and attitudes. Thoughts and attitudes are creative in the atmosphere around us. They either emit light or darkness. They are either creating chaos or order.

We make a mark on the world as we pass through, an eternal mark. We are creating a wake of either good or evil that will affect the world around us. This effect will go on in this world long after we are gone. The closer we get to the Lord, the deeper our wake for good will be and the more light we cause to shine in our world.

Adam caused evil to come into our world when he fell in the garden and his sin affected every generation since him. Similarly, our sin, if we do not deal with it, will cause an ungodly wake in our family lines, and beyond. Generations after us will be affected by it. But this wake does not have to be evil, it can be good.

Jesus left behind a tidal wave of blessing that has washed over all mankind, to all who will receive it. His life emitted enough light that He not only transcended into every realm with His salvation, He also transcended time.

A Man Sees the Spirit Realm

A wonderful man and anointed minister named Neville Johnson, whose teachings are available on the internet, had a spiritual experience that opened his eyes to how thoughts and attitudes have the ability change each person's surroundings.

Neville tells how at the beginning of his ministry the Lord opened his eyes to the spirit world. He saw the spirit realm constantly and finally begged the Lord to shut it down, which the Lord did. But during this period when his eyes were opened, Neville began to understand how we affect things in the spirit realm, and how it operates. Neville saw that every thought, word desire and emotion, is manifest through us as a power, which in the realm of the spirit is manifest with a color, a sound, a smell and even a taste. Things like love, joy, self-pity, jealousy or anger, are all visible in the spirit realm. Neville says our attitudes literally cloth us in either light or darkness.

I want to quote from Neville's online teaching called *Becoming Like Jesus Part 2,* Neville's teachings are absolutely amazing, because he comes from such an intimate walk with the Lord.

Self-pity clothes you in a terrible, dingy color and smell which keeps you bound in that state, and it affects others around you. The power coming through you will affect your health and mental state. Your attitudes clothe you in light or darkness and we all our constantly emanating something. These emanations from you are substance and have a profound effect on you.

Fear is such a strong vibration or power it can be picked up by demonic powers from a great distance. Demonic powers as well as angels can know what you are manifesting by the color, sound, smell and taste which is flowing from you.

A person's desire for good or evil manifests

power, a vibration passing through them. This light, color, sound and smell passing through you either defiles or purifies you.

Jesus said it is that which comes out of you that defiles you. Every negative, selfish, jealous, angry, unforgiving, or attitude of self-pity, is manifest this way. These attitudes will prematurely age you, cause disease and generally cause decay on every level of your existence. On the other hand, every loving, kind long suffering attitude will do the opposite and bless you with abundant life.

Getting Dressed Everyday

There is a perfect example of this in the scripture. Isaiah 61:3 tells us to put on the garment of praise for the spirit of heaviness. Now that we know this is literal, we can just imagine how ghastly the spirit of heaviness must look in the spirit realm and smell and how beautiful the garment of praise must be, it emanates light, color and a beautiful smell.

I am realizing through this how important a morning time with the Lord is, before we start our day. It is as important as getting dressed because that is exactly what it is, clothing ourselves with light before we go off to our day. We are living in a dark world, that is why it takes some effort on our part to exist in the kingdom of light in this dark world. We need to clothe ourselves with light by emanating peace, love and joy, thanksgiving and praise and other good things from the kingdom of light.

God Emits Light and Color

Do you remember how we talked earlier about the great light and colors coming off of God. God emits so much light and beautiful color because He emits so much love and joy and peace, etc. Remember our testimony from Seneca Sodi in chapter 2, here it is again,

Beyond all my power of description are the splendors around the Throne itself. As we approached nearer the entrance of the great city and to the region of the Father's throne, mighty waves of light and glory came constantly rolling over us, and with them came such refreshing baths of love, peace and joy that our gladness was indescribable, having reached a degree of perfection never known before.

Love, joy and peace are a substance in the spiritual realm, and they emit great light. The closer we walk and mirror the image of God the brighter we will become. Those who become mature in the Lord and walk in the fruit of the spirit, {which are love, joy, peace, patience, kindness, goodness, faithfulness, gentleness and self-control,} will be brighter and more beautiful in the spirit realm. There is no need there to make a pious showing of ourselves, in the spirit realm; our degree of light says it all.

Words

Words also emit different frequencies and have a huge effect on our realm and the spirit realm. Proverbs 18:21 tells us that death and life are in the power of the tongue. Again, we affect our own destiny by the words we speak. If we speak negatively over ourselves it will be impossible for us to succeed. We are releasing a negative force over ourselves which will bring negative results. If we refuse all negative words and only speak God's words over ourselves than Satan has no power to come against us. He may try but he will have nothing to work with. Instead, we come into agreement with God and release His power of good to work in our lives.

One time my husband got a trespassing ticket when he inadvertently drove on some private property. He was worried sick about it. He wondered if he would go to jail. As he was telling me about it, I felt determination come over me.

"Nothing will come of it!" I declared boldly.

Every time he would worry about it, I would declare it again. He got so worried about it he called the police station to ask him when he was supposed to come in. They told him, "Don't call us will call you." But they never did, nothing came of it. I got exactly what I spoke.

That is just a little thing, but words carry great power.

The Power of Words to Change a Life

I read a story one time about how words changed

the life of an incorrigible criminal. The story begins with Father Flanagan, who many years ago started a home for orphaned boys, called Boys Town. One night Father Flanagan received a phone call from the sheriff of another state. The sheriff asked him if he had room for another boy, immediately!

"Where is he?" father Flanagan asked the sheriff.

"In jail," the sheriff replied. "He is a desperate character," the sheriff continued, he robbed a bank and held up three stores with a revolver."

"How old is he?" asked Father Flanagan.

"Eight and a half," answered the sheriff.

The next day the sheriff and his wife arrived with the tiny hoodlum. In came a small, freckled face boy, with a mop of brown hair, eyes squinted and a lit cigarette drooping from the corner of his mouth.

The sheriff's wife handed Father Flanagan an envelope containing the boys police record and then spat out, "And that's not the half of it, this good for nothing criminal is not worth helping and it's my personal opinion he ain't even human!"

Turns out the boy's name was Eddie, just Eddie. No one knew his last name. His parents both died when Eddie was four, in a flu epidemic. From then on Eddie was passed around his neighborhood. Eddie had become boss of a gang of boys, some nearly twice his age. He browbeat them into petty crimes which he would plan out.

Father Flanagan explained to Eddie the details of staying at the boy's home and then added, "I love you and hope that someday I can take you into my heart. I know you're a good boy."

Eddie swore.

Eddie was eaten up with hate. He did not make friends at the boy's home. For many months he disrupted classes, ripped up books, and tried to escape. He would have nothing to do with baseball, football, music or the farm, nothing interested him. And nothing got through to him, no one ever saw him laugh or shed a tear.

When nothing else worked, Father Flanagan decided to try to spoil him with love. He took him on many outings that most little boys would enjoy, such as baseball games, movies and the zoo. But Eddie showed no sign of gratitude. Father Flanagan told him over and over, "Eddie you're a good boy."

But nothing seemed to get through to Eddie.

One day it all came to a head. Eddie marched into Father Flanagan's office; he wanted to have it out with Father Flanagan. For the rest of the story, I will quote the book.

"Father Flanagan, you're a phony!"

"You better prove that Eddie or shut up!"

"Okay! I just kicked a sister in the shins. Well? Now what do you say?"

"I still say you are a good boy."

"What did I tell you? You keep on saying that lie, and you know it's a lie, it can't be true—doesn't that prove you're a phony?"

Dear Father in heaven, this is honest logic! How can I answer it? How, defend my faith in him—and in you? Because it's now or never with Eddie—God give me

the grace to say the right thing.

Father Flanagan cleared his throat.

"Eddie, you're smart enough to know when a thing is really proved. What is a good boy? A good boy is an obedient boy. Right?"

"Yeah!"

"Does what his teachers tell him to do?"

"You bet!"

"Well, that's all you've ever done, Eddie. The only trouble with you is that you had the wrong teachers—wharf toughs and corner bums—but you have certainly obeyed them; you've done every last wrong and rotten thing they taught you to do. If you would obey the good teachers here in the same way, you would be just fine!"

Those simple words of unarguable truth were like an exorcism, driving devils out of the room and cleansing the air. At first the tiny human enigma looked dumbfounded. Then came a glisten of sheer, downright relief in the brown eyes, and he began to creep around the side of the sunlit desk. And with the very same relief Father Flanagan's soul was crying; he held out his arms and the child climbed into them and laid a tearful face against his heart.

That was a long time ago. For ten years Eddie remained in Boys Town, until, well near the top of his class, he left to join the United States Marines. On blood smeared beaches he won three promotions.

"His chest," boasts Father Flanagan "is covered with medals. Nothing strange about that, though; no wonder he has courage. But God be praised for

something else: he has the love of the men in his outfit—brother to the whole bunch he is –an upstanding Christian character. And still the toughest kid I ever knew!"

Father Flanagan was a man of faith. Father Flanagan kept saying Eddie was a good boy. That was not a lie. He was agreeing with God's will for the boy's life. He spoke it into existence. He created it with his words and faith and Eddie was changed forever. Eddie became a good boy.

Speaking God's will over yourself and others is the right thing to do. We can agree with our mouth that all our needs are met through Christ, that we are healed by His blood, and that God makes even our enemies to be at peace with us, and so on. Our words promote light or darkness, it is up to us.

Leaving the World a Better Place

Our thoughts, words, and attitudes have substance in the spirit realm. They emit light or darkness, color, smell and taste. Light has the power to heal and create good. Darkness destroys our health and affects others around us. We are leaving a spiritual wake as we pass through this life. A wake that will continue after we are gone. I want to leave behind a brighter world, shining with light of God, and blessing all those who are affected by my life!

Chapter Ten

Transfiguration

Now after six days Jesus took Peter, James and John his brother, led them up on a high mountain by themselves; and He transfigured before them. His face shone like the sun, and His clothes became white as light. Matthew 17:1-2

Jesus, like the Father is a being of light. While Jesus walked on earth, He appeared to be a regular human being. But His spirit man was covered with His human flesh. So that is what the people on earth at that time saw, was human flesh. But Jesus, the Son of God, is the exact image of God, He is that same light.

Peter, James and John saw Jesus transfigure before them. They saw Jesus in His true form, light and the source of all light. His face became brighter than the sun and His clothes as white as light. They saw what was hiding under that human flesh, LIGHT! The Light of Jesus is that eternal, uncreated light. John 1:9 tells us, *Jesus is the true Light that gives light to every man coming into the world*.

Peter, James and John weren't all that saw the true light of Jesus while He was on earth the demons saw His light and were tormented by it. In Matthew 8:28-29 we get a little picture of this.

When He had come to the other side to the country of the Gergesenes there met Him two demon possessed men coming out of the tombs, exceedingly fierce so that no one could pass that way. And suddenly they cried out saying, "What have we to do with You, Jesus, You Son of God? Have You come to torment us before our time?"

There is nothing more tormenting to darkness than light! Devils and demons cannot stand the light of God. They could see Jesus as a being of light, and they cried out because of it.   Jesus is pure light that darkness cannot stand!

His light, God's light is at a frequency that is undetected by human eyes. Remember only a very small amount of light's frequencies are detectable by the human eye. There is so much we don't see. Every kind of light has a certain frequency. Of course, God's light is the highest form of light and has the most divine frequency; He is light in the brightest and highest form. Jesus is brighter than the noon sun. The apostle John in his vision of Jesus describes Jesus in Revelation 1:13-18, he says, *And in the midst of the seven lampstands One like the Son of man, clothed with a garment down to the feet and girded about the chest with a golden band. His head and hair were white like wool, as white as snow, and His eyes like a flame of fire; His feet were like fine brass, as if refined in a furnace, and His voice as the sound of many waters; he had in His right hand seven stars, out of his mouth went a sharp two edged sword, and His countenance was like the sun shining in its strength. "*

Try looking at the summer sun at midday. It is too bright to do. Jesus is brighter than that.

I have also read many modern-day testimonies of people who have seen Jesus in His glory; Jesse Duplantis in his book, *Heaven Close Encounters of the God Kind,* described his heavenly vision of Jesus in his book,"

To me He looked like a shaft of light. He was so glorious. I stood and looked at Him. There was a brilliance coming out of Him that seemed like waves of glory. The light was emanating from Him. His clothes were beautiful and looked like solid diamonds that were sparkling. Jesus was taller than I thought He would be. I would guess Him to be from five feet eleven inches to six feet one inch. I thought at first His hair was white; but when He turned His head, I caught a glance and saw that it was light brown. When He looked at me, the glory of God was emanating from Him.

Jesse is seeing Jesus as the three on the mount saw Him, as He really is. Another testimony of the appearance of Jesus is described beautifully by Anna Rountree in her book The *Heavens Opened.* Anna sees Jesus on the path ahead of her and she describes it.

Immediately ahead of us on the path was a burning light. Hundreds of spirits surrounded His

brilliance, darting in and lifting out like eagles catching heat currents. They were flying with the light as if escorting it. So bright was this intense light that it reduced the spirits to silver outlines of themselves in its radiance. It reminded me of figures passing in front of bright headlights on a dark night, although there were no surrounding darkness. Everything paled that was near this intense brightness.

All these witnesses describe the light of Jesus. Jesus is intense brightness and glory. This is His true form.

The Shroud of Turin

I have always believed in the authenticity of the shroud of Turin. If you have never heard of the Shroud of Turin, it is a fourteen-foot-long burial cloth believed by many to be the actual burial cloth of Jesus. This cloth has an image on it of a man with the identical wounds that Jesus had. He has wounds around His forehead where the cross of thorns would have been. The man was also whipped; the flesh on His back has been whipped and is torn to shreds. He has been crucified, there are nail prints in his wrists and ankles, and he has a spear wound in his side. His face has been beaten and His beard has even been torn.

Another reason why I believe its authenticity is because the man looks like Jesus. I have seen Him with my physical eyes, and He looked very much like this man. He had a prominent nose and deep-set eyes, high cheek bones and a high forehead. So does the image of the man on the shroud!

Many experts and scientists have done innumerable number of tests on the shroud, and they have concluded a few things. The shroud is not a picture, it is a negative. The shroud is like a giant three dimensional negative. The shroud has not been painted or dyed and the blood on the shroud is genuine.

The cloth itself also appears to be genuine. It is typical of the burial cloths from Jesus' period of time and the pollen found in the shroud comes from plants found in the Middle East.

The real mystery of the shroud is how the image was imprinted, which to me is not that hard to figure out! I believe the image was burned onto the shroud by the immense flash of light that occurred when Jesus re-entered His body and rose from the dead. A powerful flash of light occurred when Jesus rose from the dead. The light was so bright it left a negative image on Jesus' burial cloth. A perfect negative of His image and the wounds on His body! Remember we learned that light is energy and power. Something immense happened here.

There is a reason I want you to think about the power and brightness that was released in this great miracle of Jesus 'resurrection, because it is personal to you! This resurrection power is the same power God has placed in you!

Therefore I also, after I heard of your faith in the Lord Jesus and your love for all the saints, do not cease to give thanks to God for you, making mention of you in my prayers: That the God of our Lord Jesus Christ, the Father of glory, may give you the spirit of wisdom and revelation in the knowledge of Him, the eyes of your spirit being enlightened; that you may know the hope of his calling, what are the riches of His glory of his inheritance of the saints, and what is the **exceeding greatness of his power toward us who believe, according to the working of his mighty power which He worked in Christ when He raised him from the dead and seated Him at his right hand in the heavenly places,** *Ephesians 1:15-20*

I have been crucified with Christ; it is no longer I who live, but Christ lives in me; and the life which I now live in the flesh I live by faith in the Son of God, who loved me and gave Himself for me. Galatians 2:20

We have had something powerful happen on the inside of us. We have had a death and resurrection on the inside of us. We have been crucified with Christ and now Christ lives in us. This is the same power that raised Jesus Christ from the dead. There is something living in us who have truly come to the Lord. LIGHT!!! We have His light in us. The same light, the same power, it is the same frequency as the power that raised Jesus from the dead; it is the same frequency as Jesus because He lives inside us. We have literally become beings of light!

Superpower

I recently heard a sermon on the internet, by Bruce Allen. Bruce Allen is a minister who frequently talks about translation, being transported from one place to another. This is something the early church experienced, and Bruce Allen has had this experience also.

In his sermon Bruce was talking about how God told him to study light. After he had studied light for a while, he had an experience in the spirit realm where he actually pulled back what he called the garments of the flesh and looked down at his chest. He said it reminded him of Clark Kent pulling back his suit and finding out he was superman. As Bruce opened up his garment of flesh and looked down at his chest, he saw a bright ray of light. He realized that his spirit man was light. He was shining brightly; he was made of light.

God told him, "This is who you are."

Later Elijah appeared to Bruce and told him he was there to show Bruce how to enter heaven without dying. Elijah put out his hand and it became light. Then he told Bruce to do it. Bruce faltered at first but then did it. Like Elijah's hand Bruce's also became light.

In the form of light, he could travel at the speed of thought and go forward and backwards through time. This is mind bending stuff. I believe God is raising up a supernatural church!

When we are told we are light in scripture this isn't a figurative way of describing us, this is literal, this is spiritual truth. We are light. We are not just any light we are Christs light. This is our spirit man, conformed to the image of Christ.

When we see Jesus as He really is, we will see Him shining in amazing light. As we become conformed to his image we will begin to shine brighter and brighter. This is who we are in Christ!

We have to remember our salvation is not totally complete yet. Our bodies are going to go through a transformation. They will become resurrected bodies much like Jesus. The Bible speaks of a resurrection that is yet to come.

For the Lord Himself will descend from heaven with a shout, with the voice of an archangel, and with the trumpet of God. And the dead in Christ will rise first. Then we who are still alive and remain shall be caught up together with them in the clouds to meet the Lord in the air. And thus, we shall always be with the Lord.1 Thessalonians 5:28

Even the people in heaven do not have a resurrected body yet. We have a new body coming that will resurrect like Jesus body did. They will be glorious. We will undergo a transformation, which has already begun in us. We have become beings of light with the resurrection power of Jesus in our spirits and soon our bodies will follow!

Chapter Eleven

The Truth and Lies

Lying lips are an abomination to the Lord, but those who deal truthfully are His delight. Proverbs 12:22

Lies are like spider webs; we weave a deception, and we get caught in them ourselves. I know. I have had my share of lying and getting caught up in webs.

When I was in High School, in my senior year I signed up for a program to work and get credit for school. My dad had provided my sister and I with an old jalopy to share so I had transportation. I got a job and was all set to start but my mother's car broke down, so she took off in the jalopy and went out of town for a week.

I couldn't believe my mother did this to me and I didn't know how to handle it. I was left with a new job and no way to get there. My then boyfriend, {now husband} who was older than I was, had a car I could use but I had to wait for him to get out of work to use it. He got out at 3pm and I was supposed to be at work at 2pm. I didn't want to tell my new employer the whole story so I told them I would be late for the first week or so because my brother needed the car. I thought it sounded better than the real story.

So, I made up this brother that didn't exist who was really Jim, my boyfriend. So, everyone at work thought I had a brother. Then my mom came home, and I had the car back and I started talking at work about my boyfriend. So, half the time when I was at work and I talked about Jim, he was my brother and half the time he was my boyfriend. I was starting to get mixed up myself. I never used his name, I just said, my brother, or my boyfriend. But the lie kind of grew. The better I got to know these people the worse it felt. Then after a few months of this mess Jim came in to bring me lunch and some of my co-workers said, "Was that your brother or your boyfriend?"

I finally said, "Both." And I explained the whole thing. I was tired of lying!

There have been many times I have lied out of fear. I hate confrontation. When I first got married, I soon learned that my new husband was MEAN!!!! He had such a bad temper, and I was a mouse. He ruled the roost. {at first] He told me I was never ever to cook using onions. He hated onions. I was absolutely forbidden. Well, I love onions. Life without onions was a dismal thought. So, I just cut the onions up so small that I knew he would never even know they were there.

One night I had made spaghetti and Jim, and I were sitting at the table eating, when suddenly he pounded his fist on the table. His face got red and contorted with anger. He bellowed at me, "Did you put onions in this spaghetti??!!!??!!! I told you no onions!!!!"

My first thought was to bolt out the door and try to find a homeless shelter to live in. But I just sat there shaking and in my best voice I could muster I simply said, "No honey, there are no onions in here."

"Oh," he said his face returning to normal, and then continued eating. Years later I confessed. But things have changed in our house. My big grump has become a pussy cat. I now brazenly put onions in his food and if he doesn't like it, oh well. The other day he was making chili. I asked him if he was going to put any onions in it and he said, "No."

"Don't expect me to eat it then."

He put great big pieces of onions in it.

Well, anyway, at first, I was so scared of Jim, I lied a lot. The problem with lying is it takes your peace away, and it grieves the Holy Spirit within you. It is something we need to really work on. It is really horrible. It has no place in the kingdom of light and God never lies!

God and the Truth

God will never, ever lie. Once He speaks something it becomes so. Once it is spoken by Him it can't be changed. Many people think of God like a dictator, "after all He is God, He can do whatever He wants," they say.

God does not do whatever He wants. He doesn't operate like that. He obeys laws. He honors His word.

Once He speaks it becomes so, He will not go back on His word. We have no concept of His level of truth because we do not function on His level. We say things we don't mean all the time. We have no idea the power of words or the value of truth. God does.

God will not lie; neither will He take back what He has given to you. He has made you an eternal being; you won't ever cease to exist. He has also given you a free will. You have the power to choose your eternal destiny by the choices you make. He will honor your choice to reject Him if that is what you choose. He will not infringe on the rights He has given you. This would make Him untruthful. That doesn't mean that He wants you to go to Hell. Absolutely not! He made a legal way for your salvation, and He paid a very high price for it!

Satan is a Liar

Satan on the other hand operates treacherously. He lies, he steals, and he kills. If you think you will ever get anything good from the kingdom of darkness, you won't. Jesus surprised the religious leaders when he told them, *"You are of your father the devil, and the desires of your father you want to do. He was a murderer from the beginning, and does not stand in the truth, because there is no truth in him. When he speaks a lie, he speaks from his own resources, for he is a liar and the father of it." John 8:44*

So, all you are going to get from the kingdom of

darkness are lies, but you will never get lies from God. Lying, deceit and twisting the truth are the way Satan operates. Even those who devoutly follow him, those who serve him, think he will honor his promises to them. They will find they are sadly mistaken; any promise from him was a lie, he speaks no truth.

Characteristics of the Truth and of Lies

Generally the truth can be stated simply. Liars need a lot of words. They need to talk and talk to twist and twist their words.

Liars twist the scriptures to say something else.

Liars make themselves an exception to the rule. They have to. So, they can do what they want.

Liars hate the truth. It enrages them. They persecute the truth.

Liars are pushy. No matter how much they accuse those who love truth that they are intolerant, they are the ones who are intolerant, but only of the truth.

Liars operate under Satan's rule, they operate out of hate there is no love there.

Liars are bold and brash; they are in rebellion standing against God. Sinners are liars because they have something to hide.

Liars also lie to themselves.

A lie is anything Satan says although there may be a bit of truth in it.

Lies grieve the Holy Spirit, they oppose God.

Truth needs no defense; it can simply be stated.

Truth always wins out in the end.

Truth can appear narrow-minded because lies can be plentiful but there is only one truth.

Truth is worth defending.

The Bible is true.

Truth is anything that God says.

Truth is eternal, lies are temporary.

Truth sets us free.

I am going to expose some of the lies of our times. Let's start with,

Religion

There is a big lie that struts around masquerading as the truth, and that is religion. Religion pretends to be the way to God but in reality, it has persecuted those who belong to God all through the ages. In fact, it was the religious leaders who persecuted and then finally killed Jesus. It is no different today.

Very few churches today let the Holy Spirit lead the service. Even a lot of so-called Pentecostal services do not allow the Holy Spirit to operate. I went to a spirit filled church in my area that was having a revival meeting. They had a special speaker invited. After the worship time the guest speaker spoke and then after he spoke, he started to pray. As he was praying the Holy Spirit fell. No one moved to leave because the atmosphere was charged, and the people started spontaneously worshipping.

This is when Church can really start to get good. Miracles will happen because that is the Holy Spirits will for us. I could feel that something wonderful was about to happen. Then the pastor got up and dismissed the service! I could not believe it! The time was up so he was done!

Even though the pastor had dismissed the people, the people were reluctant to leave there was such a wonderful presence there, but he shooed us out. This was a religious spirit in operation. It opposed the true move of God because it would mean that church would have gotten out late. I have been in great meetings that have lasted until 2am!!!!They are led by the Holy Spirit and time means nothing.

Religion and the true spirit of God are in opposition. And it is religion that keeps millions of people from following the truth because it poses as the truth, but it is an empty shell. There is a true church and a false church set up on the earth. One is a form, and one is true. Be sure you belong to the true.

There is coming a religion that will persecute all true believers. It will be the "Love Generation." They accept everyone. Homosexuality will be welcomed, along with every other kind of perversion. Anyway, to God will be accepted, except the true way, the blood of Jesus Christ. But those who hold fast to the real truth will be branded intolerant and hateful.

Religion is the enemy of the truth and had been all through the ages. Some of the most hideous tortures have been carried out on true believers by the religious leaders of the times. Look at the Middle Ages and their implements of torture. This was the false religion versus the true church.

Atheists and Evolutionists

Some of the most ludicrous theories have been concocted and passed off to the world as believable. One such is evolution. To believe in evolution one would have to be crazy. When I was in High School it was taught as fact. No mention of creation was even given. Evolution is so ridiculous even evolutionists don't believe it themselves.

Kent Hovind, an opponent to evolution often will debate evolutionists. Although Kent is a controversial figure and has legal problems, I loved watching his videos.

One time he was debating evolutionists on the truth to Noah's ark. One of the team of men opposing Kent asked him how Noah fit all the animals on the ark, such as dogs there are so many breeds of dogs. Kent told him there were only two dogs on the ark, all the dogs and breeds on the earth came from those two breeds. The man debating him said you mean to suggest that all the breeds came from only two dogs?!

Kent was amazed, this was an evolutionist, and he didn't believe dogs could breed dogs?!! Dogs can breed other dogs, but they will never breed monkeys or men!!! He obviously couldn't be too serious about his evolution beliefs if he had trouble with dogs. Evolution is a perpetuated lie.

Science is now coming up with more evidence that proves God. I personally don't care if they do, or if they don't. I don't need science to prove God for me to believe the Bible or that God exists. I never have.

But if someone needs proof then I think the best proof is creation itself. It is so incredibly complex and precise. Every bit of creation, from energy, to matter, time and space, to nature all around us, our human bodies, plants and animals etc. etc., everything is so intricately and marvelously made, that not only does it cause me to believe in God, it causes me to realize that God is so much greater than any of us could possibly fathom. We are in for a real shock when we see Him face to face and realize He is so much greater than our imaginations can comprehend.

Evolutionists and atheists that come up with these ridiculous lies and promote them, leave themselves no hope. They spend their lives pushing lies. I think it is very interesting to read some of these prominent atheists and evolutionists' last words that they utter before dying. In fact, I will quote some for you.

Voltaire, one of history's best-known atheists cried out on his death bed, "I am abandoned by God and man! I shall go to hell! O, Jesus Christ!"

Clarence Darrow, the scopes trial lawyer, he asked several clergymen, while he was dying, "Please intercede for me with the Almighty. During my life I have spoken many times against Christians and now I realize I may have been wrong."

Sir Thomas Scott, "Until now I thought there was no God or hell. Now I know there is both, and I am doomed."

Sir Julian Huxley, evolutionist and staunch atheist, "So it is true after all, so it is true after all."

David Hume, the atheist died crying out, "I am in flames."

Sir Francis Newport, the head of an English infidel club, "I know I am lost forever! Oh, that fire! Oh, the insufferable pangs of hell!"

Thomas Carlyle, "I am as good as without hope, a sad old man gazing into the final chasm."

Thomas Paine, who wrote *The Age of Reason*, which viewed the Bible as ordinary literature., "I would give worlds if I had them…… that *The Age of Reason* had never been published. Oh God, save me; for I am at the edge of hell, alone…"

These are the last words of those who spent their lives promoting these lies. Their ends were hopeless and that is all they can offer to those who follow their works, hopelessness. They trade the truth for cleverly or not so cleverly crafted lies. They lead others to the same hopeless states as they have led themselves.

Abortion

Abortion is insanity. It is not just the murder of another human being. It is the murder of an innocent, helpless human being.

But its promoters never mention a baby. They call themselves pro-choice. The choice they are so pro about is the choice to slaughter an innocent life.

It is a sickening lie.

We can still have the choice not to have children without taking a life, and once a life is established, we can choose to give the baby up for adoption. But murder is not a choice, it is a crime.

Some folks believe in the middle somewhere they believe it is okay to murder a child who was conceived by rape, making the innocent child pay for the crime with his life. Even so, to kill that child would still be murder!

Liars are Everywhere

I cannot believe how many people are making their living off lies and deceit. They are everywhere. How about the mail? There are so many scams out there. They are targeting the seniors, mostly. I have read lots of it. I have seen many of the elderly people I have worked for being taken for thousands of dollars through scams in the mail. They promise that you have won a huge prize, but you have to send in money to claim it. Or they sell you a priceless heirloom that is worthless. One of those commemorative coins being sold for twenty-five dollars, it turned out was worth about a penny.

And then there are the phone scams. I got a call and they said they were the IRS and they wanted money from me. I knew I didn't owe them any money. I talked to several others who got the same call. My son called the IRS to inquire about it, they told him they never call, they only send letters. Or have you gotten your call yet that you won a free cruise?

And how about the millions being scammed on the internet? Widows being targeted on dating sites by supposed lovers who talk them out of every dime they have. And that is just one of the scams, there are many, many more.

Anytime you sell someone anything, misrepresenting what it is just to get someone's money; that is a lie. Investment brokers do it, real estate brokers do it, and infomercials do it. We are living in treacherous times. Liars are rampant. It is listed as one of the sins in the book of Revelations. It is one of the sins of the end times.

*But the cowardly, unbelieving, abominable, murderers, sexually immoral, sorcerers, idolaters and **all liars** shall have their part in the lake of fire and brimstone which is the second death. Revelation 21:8*

Lie Busters

I want to quickly go through some of the lies of our

times. I am not going to give you a big, long explanation on each topic because this is a mini lie buster. There may be some Christians that disagree with me, but this is the way I see it. I just want to lay down a basis for truth, for some these things may be a no brainer but for others it may be eye opening. These are kind of random and plentiful but here goes....

Gambling—it is ill gotten gain and will cause a curse, if you win, but if you lose, what a waste of money!

Marijuana—it is not medicine; it is a very demonic drug.

Alcohol—I will never believe it is okay! Do you know how many people have suffered from alcohol? Whether as alcoholics themselves or the victims of abuse from those who drink? I am one of them and I hate the miserable stuff!!! I don't care if you drink it in moderation! Don't cause your brother to stumble!!

Pornography—it is destructive to the person who looks at it, to their marriage, and to society as a whole. Pornography is extremely demonic. The Bible tells us two things will never be satisfied, lust and the grave. Don't feed lust, you will have to feed again and again.

Homosexuality—the Bible is clear on it; it is an abomination.

Horoscopes—the whole thing is demonic and opens you up to that realm, leave it alone and that goes for fortune tellers' psychics and anything along those lines. We can only receive revelation about the future from one source, the Holy Spirit, and the avenues through which He speaks. Jesus promised us the Holy Spirit would tell us the things to come.

Profanity—it feeds the dark realm.

Euthanasia—Thou shall not kill*!* I believe the time is coming when anyone who is not useful will be "put to sleep" Obamacare is the beginning of that.

Gun Control—to give up our second amendment rights is suicide. Then only your enemies will be armed!

Modified genetics or embryonic stem cell research—Don't mess with this stuff! God destroyed the pre flood generation that messed with DNA. And harvesting humans for research, how hideous!

Money Grabbing Televangelists—Television ministers need to pay their bills and it is okay to support them, but that is not how you get a prayer answered! I love it that the gospel is preached on television, it is awesome. But it is not the gospel that we have to send money to receive a miracle, it is by faith we receive, not coercion.

Where Can We Go for Truth?

We have a book filled with truth, the Bible! There are answers for our lives there. As we read it some things in our lives will have to change. We have to line ourselves up with the truth. The Bible is a lamp unto out feet and a light unto our path.

And Jesus said, "I am the Way the Truth and the Life." Jesus is truth. We need a relationship with the Lord and to walk with Him. His words are truth, we can live by them. His example is truth, we can follow His example.

Jesus left earth so He could send us the Holy Spirit. Jesus promised the Holy Spirit would guide us into all truth. Learning to follow the guiding of the Holy Spirit will protect you from the pitfalls of life. Liars are everywhere and He will protect you. Ask Him for help. If we learn to follow the voice of the Holy Spirit, we will not be deceived. He will alert you to trouble. He will even warn you of trouble coming that you know nothing about.

One time my mother was renting out a house she owned. A woman came to see the house and the minute she walked in I felt an invisible wave hit me. I said to myself, "Yuk." I felt repulsed.

I thought I was being judgmental, but it was a warning from the Holy Spirit. That woman moved in with her family and never paid the rent. They also did a lot of damage to the house. I hadn't learned to recognize the Holy Spirit's warning yet.

Since then, He has helped me avoid trouble many times. I have been in situations that are confusing. He will show me in a dream exactly what is going on. Many times, it has even been for someone else. One time a friend of mine was dating a man she met at the singles club in church. She was going to marry him. I had a dream that he was an animal that kept changing forms, but I knew in the dream his true form was a rat. Sometimes he would look cute and cuddly, but he was really a rat. I told her the dream, and I prayed like crazy! Thank goodness she didn't marry him, but he married another woman from the church and after he took her money he disappeared. God gave my husband an opportunity to warn the lady that married him beforehand, but she wouldn't listen. She paid a heavy price.

The Holy Spirit has also helped us when buying a used car, {the only kind of car I have ever bought}.

Because I don't know anything about cars sometimes, he will just tell me the color and make of the car I am supposed to buy.

The voice of the Holy Spirit is very gentle. It is often times very easy to miss. It takes work to learn to follow Him. It takes laying aside your own will and being willing to hear what He wants. Many times, it will oppose what we naturally want.

The Most Important Thing in Life

The biggest truth we can have in our lives is to have our priorities straight, to put things in our lives in order of most importance and live our lives accordingly. The most important thing in your life and your biggest need is your relationship with Jesus Christ, Your Savior and only hope. Next would be your marriage. Now comes your children.

Having said that I want to make a point because many people get divorced, and marry someone else, who are not the parent of your child. I am tired of seeing children abused by a stepparent. If you divorce, and have small children, then you have a different situation. You cannot bring someone into your home that will not love your child as their own or will mistreat that child in any way. The protection and well-being of your dependent child, {not adult child} has to be a priority, before a second marriage.

After our big priorities, we now have priorities of our extended family, our church, our jobs and to those God puts in our paths. We want to prove faithful in all these things.

Summing it all Up

I think I had better begin summing up this chapter on truth and lies before it becomes a whole book. So, we see truth belongs on the side of light and lies will always be on the side of darkness. We have come out of darkness where lying was second nature, but this is no longer okay. We now realize that as children of light, lying has no place in our lives. We also live in a world where lies have run rampant. We need to hang onto the truth with everything we have got. Our source of truth is the Bible, God's word, and God, Himself in the persons of the Father, Jesus and the Holy Spirit. Speaking anything but the truth grieves the Holy Spirit. We need to value the truth and put away lies.

Chapter Twelve

Taking Off the Blindfolds

If then you were raised with Christ, seek those things which are above, where Christ is, sitting at the right hand of God. Set your mind on things above, not on things of earth. Colossians 3:2

I think about heaven and hell a lot. I think everyone should think about it. We need to get to heaven, and we need to stay out of hell. There is nothing on earth worth going to hell for; therefore, thinking about it often keeps me serious about eternity. There is nothing more serious to think about than eternity.

One time, I saw on television, the restaurant camera footage of Princess Diana and her boyfriend Dodi Fayed minutes before they died. They were standing in a hallway apparently planning their exit carefully so as to avoid the cameras that followed them everywhere. Little did they know that in a few short minutes their lives on earth would be over. One minute they were here and the next minute time for them had stopped forever.

Keeping an Eternal Perspective

Life can be over unexpectedly for anyone. Sometimes, when life is really getting me down because I can't seem to get everything done that I need to get done, or I wonder how I am going to keep up the pace I am keeping until my retirement years because my body is slowing down, then I think of Princess Diana and Dodi Fayed in that hallway. It seemed like just another day, but it was their last minutes.

Then I think of my life and leaving it, all of it and never returning. I think what if these were my last minutes. Suddenly the things I am worried about don't seem important at all, and different things seem important. Suddenly the least important on my list is temporal things, and the most important are the eternal things.

We need to take inventory from an eternal perspective periodically. We need to continually evaluate our lives, bearing in mind that this could be the last day we live. It is not being morbid or gruesome, it is wisdom. We need to be prepared for our dying day. Millions of people enter hell every day and live an eternity with regret. At that point the only thing that matters to anyone is faith in the Lord Jesus Christ. It didn't seem important while they were on earth. Suddenly it is the only thing of importance, and they have to live for eternity with regret.

It is equally important to those of us, who have our faith in the Lord Jesus Christ, to continually realize its importance. He is to be the main focus of our life. Nothing, nothing, nothing, is more important. Nothing comes close to it when we have an eternal perspective. This is part of living in the kingdom of light and living with an eternal perspective.

Darkness Blinds Us to an Eternal Perspective

It is the work of darkness to blind the minds of humans from thinking about eternal things. The Bible tells us this, In *2 Corinthians 4:3 But even if our gospel is veiled, it is veiled to those who are perishing, whose minds the god of this age has blinded, who do not believe, lest the light of the Gospel of the glory of Christ, who is the image of God, should shine on them.*

It is the job of the prince of the power of the air to blind the minds of those on earth to the truth of the gospel. The work of darkness will keep the focus of people on the lusts of their flesh, and empty things that will keep your focus off what is important, until it is too late.

Satan uses many different mind sets. One such mind set is to live a good life. It goes something like this: work hard in school and get good grades, so you can go to college and get a good education, so you can get a good job. Marry well and make lots of money so you can have a nice home and nice children. Surround yourself with beautiful things, have a nice well-kept home with beautiful furniture and a nice lawn, and be sure to drive a nice car. Take nice vacations every year and be sure to save a lot of money so you can enjoy a nice retirement, preferably in Florida or Arizona. Work hard and do all the right things so you can have a nice life! Does that sound so bad? That doesn't sound so evil, does it? That life is totally focused on earth. That life is not prepared for eternity; it has left out the most important thing.

That is only one such mindset. There are many more. Some are much more fleshly. Some worship themselves. They make beauty a priority. They exercise their bodies daily, so they look their very best, they spend money on the finest clothes, and their hair is big priority, the beauty shop is regular stop, so that their hair is always in the latest style, for the men or woman. They have an expensive ring on their finger, and they may live in a dump, but the car has to be flashy. Now comes the fun part, luring the opposite sex, or for some the same sex. Going from partner to partner, relationship to relationship, whoever tickles their fancy for the moment. They may marry, but they won't be faithful, they can't waste all that beauty on one person.

Or how about the party animal? They waste their lives on alcohol or drugs. They may plan on quitting someday, but not today. Many of these people die very young, in their teens even, they die of overdoses. Suddenly they are in hell; they thought they were invincible, but many find out too late, they weren't.

Oh but there are so many more mind-sets to keep our focus off eternal things, there is fame, wealth, sex, violence and crime, power, education and intellectualism, worshipping the mind, the occult, false religions, even self-pity all these mind- sets, that can preoccupy a life until it is too late.

A Man's Experiment in Prayer

Kenneth Hagin tells in his book, *Ministering to Your Family*, of learning about this as he was reading his Bible. He saw in 2 Corinthians 4, as he was reading one day, that the god of this world had blinded the minds of those who were lost. God began to speak to him, He asked Kenneth, "Do you think a sane sensible person would drive his car down the highway at 80 to 100 miles an hour, run right by flashing lights and signs that said, 'Danger Ahead' or 'Bridge Out' and run off the road and kill himself?"

Kenneth answered, "No."

Then Kenneth realized a drunk or doped person would because his mind is blinded. Similarly, the devil has blinded the minds of the unsaved because no rational human being would race through life and plunge into hell!

Kenneth realized something he had never thought of before: *We need to break the power of the devil over our unsaved loved ones, because the devil has their mind blinded*! Kenneth decided to try it out and he decided to try it in the hardest place first, his brother Dub. He reasoned, "If I can make it work on my brother Dub, I can make it work on anybody, because he's the black sheep of the family. Many of them are sinners but he is the worst case. If it will work on Dub, it will work on ANYBODY!"

Kenneth had already been praying and fasting for his brother, Dub, for fifteen years but nothing seemed to work. This was new. He lifted up his Bible in one hand and lifted his other hand to heaven. He prayed, "In the name of the Lord Jesus Christ, I break the power of the devil over my brother Dub's life, and I claim his deliverance. That means full deliverance from the devil and full salvation in Jesus' name. Amen."

Kenneth decided that prayer settled it for him. He wasn't even going to think about it again or pray anymore. It was settled.

After about a week went by, a voice said to Kenneth, "Oh, come on now. You don't really believe old Dub will ever be saved, do you?"

Kenneth knew that as long as Satan can get us into a battle with reason, he will whip us every time, but if Kenneth kept the battle in faith, he would defeat Satan every time. Kenneth answered, "No, I don't think Dub will be saved, I know Dub will be saved. You see, Satan I broke your power over Dub and claimed his deliverance— deliverance and full salvation." Then Kenneth shut his mind off and refused to worry about it.

Within two weeks Dub was saved! At the time Kenneth was writing the story his brother Dub was preaching!

Once Kenneth's brother Dub's mind was no longer blinded by the Satan, he got saved. He could see the reality of his spiritual condition, he was no longer blinded, and the light of the gospel of Christ was plain for him to see.

Al Anon and Alcoholism

AA and Al Anon work on God's principles and that is why it works. I started going to Al Anon not because I wanted to go but because God wanted me to go. I was too religious; I thought that I just wanted to pray about it instead of going to a non-church group. But eventually after being married to an alcoholic husband for many years I started to go.

In Al Anon we learn about something that keeps the alcoholic drinking called "denial." Denial is the mind blinder. Al Anon doesn't see it as a spirit, but that is how I see it. It is an evil force that keeps the alcoholic drinking because they deny there is a problem.

It is crucial that the spouses and families learn about and understand denial. It is the key to helping the alcoholic. Because our natural tendency is to fix everything that the alcoholic does wrong, this keeps the alcoholic locked in denial. Then our other natural tendency is to nag, complain, scream and go crazy, which also keeps the alcoholic in denial. The alcoholic says to himself, "I am not the one with the problem, she is."

Once we the families of alcoholics understand about denial and how to stop our part in the denial problem, things begin to change.

First, we stop trying to change them and leave them to God. Then we focus on our own problems and flaws and focus on our own relationship with God. And most of all we stop fixing the alcoholics problems. If they throw up all over the place, we don't clean it up, of course, before AL Anon my husband would never even see his mess. I would have it cleaned up before he woke up. Then he denied it happened. We are taught that an alcoholic needs to experience the pain of his actions in order to wake up from denial. We can't fix their life anymore.

It is a little harder than you think because I had to let my husband lose his job. He had gotten a good job as a meat cutter at a good supermarket. His first year there was learning the job and after a year, the salary doubled. My husband, Jim, had been training for a year and was almost to the point of a really good paying job, with every benefit. That would have meant so much to me! I was delivering 500 newspapers every night seven days a week. I could have quit my job, I was tired.

One night Jim had drank so much that when it came time for work the next morning, he was still drunk. I thought about just calling in and telling his job he was sick and then making sure he didn't go in like that. But I didn't. Jim went in and lost his job. In fact, Jim has never had a job as good as that job again ever. It was hard.

Did he quit drinking? No, just the opposite, without a job he drank so heavily I didn't see him for days and didn't even know where he was. But he did know he had a problem. The denial was gone. Within a month he checked himself into a hospital and was gone for four months. He successfully completed his program. That was an accomplishment even though it was many more years before he was able to maintain sobriety. There are things that are much more important than a good job with benefits, and that is a person's eternal well-being.

Once the denial is gone most alcoholics will get sober. It is the mind blinder again! Once they see their true condition, change is just around the corner. In fact, the statistics we learned in Al Anon were that 97% of all alcoholics will die drunk, go insane or wind up in prison. Those whose families get help and learn how to stop covering for them, have much better odds, their odds of getting better go up to 87%. It is no wonder God was so determined that I go to Al-Anon.

The Cares of Life

Since the fall of Adam the world lies under the power of the evil one. The earth is covered with his darkness; there is a thick cloud of his depression and hopelessness that is growing darker. If we keep our eyes focused on this world and what it has to offer, we can easily be caught up in the cares of this life which will choke out our faith and our spiritual life. In Matthew 13, in the Parable of the Sower, we learn that the seed that falls among the thorns is the cares of the world.

Now he who received the seed among the thorns is he who hears the word and the cares of this world, and the deceitfulness of riches choke the word, and he becomes unfruitful. Matthew 13:22

The cares of this world are a big part of the blinders that the kingdom of darkness uses to blind us from spiritual things. The cares of the world are the rat race that we all can so easily get caught up in. We think everything has to be "just so." It is also the mindset of stock piling money so that we will always have what we need.

My problem with that is I don't have the ability to make money. I have scratched out a living my whole life. And when I do get some money saved, a few good disasters like my car breaking down, or surgery, can wipe out years of saving! What a rat race!!!!

The cares of this world have been my biggest stumbling block in my life! I keep thinking my problems are something a whole lot of money would fix! Now there is part two of the verse, the deceitfulness of riches.

Have you ever daydreamed of winning a game show, and then planned every penny of what you would spend? I have so many things that need doing around my house that I don't think there is a game show that exists that could give me enough money.

I have problems around here, my cupboard doors keep falling off in my kitchen. I have put them back up so many times they won't stay up anymore. First it was just one cupboard door, so I put up a little curtain. Now it is four cupboard doors and two kitchen drawers that have bit the dust. My kitchen is a comical sight. But the cupboard doors are not the first thing on my list to get fixed. There are three or four big projects before it! My bathroom floor needs to be replaced and the shed in the backyard is about to fall down!

I keep thinking my only problem is lack of money, but it is not. My problem is the cares of this world. My cupboard doors, my floors or my shed are not as big of problems as they seem to me. In fact, they are small.

Jesus gave us the cure to the cares of life; it is in the Bible. I am going to give you some scripture that I am sure you have already heard, but if you are like me, you need to really get a hold of it, because it is the answer to a problem that is tough to beat, the cares of life.

"Do not lay up for yourselves treasures on earth, where moth and rust destroy and where thieves break in and steal; but lay up for yourselves treasures in heaven, where neither moth nor rust destroys and where thieves do not break in and steal. For where your treasure is your heart will be also." Matthew 6:22-23

"Therefore I say to you, do not worry about your life, what you will eat or what you will drink; nor about the body, what you will put on. Is not life more than food and the body more than clothing? Look at the birds of the air, for they neither sow nor reap nor gather into barns; yet your heavenly Father feeds them. Are you not of more value than they? Which of you by worrying can add one cubit to his stature? So why do you worry about clothing? Consider the lilies of the field, how they grow: they neither toil nor spin; and yet I say to you that even Solomon in all his glory was not arrayed like one of these. Now if God so clothes the grass of the field, which today is, and tomorrow is thrown into the oven, will He not much more clothe you, O you of little faith?

Therefore, do not worry, saying, 'What shall we eat? or What shall we drink? or What shall we wear?' For after all these things the Gentiles seek. For your heavenly

Father knows that you need all these things. But seek first the kingdom of God and His righteousness, and all these things shall be added unto you. Therefore, do not worry about tomorrow, for tomorrow will worry about its own things. Sufficient for today is its own trouble." Matthew 6:25-34

This is the solution to avoiding the cares of this world. First of all, our wealth needs to be stored up in heaven, not on earth. Our value in this life is to be on eternal things and not the very temporary. So, this is a huge focus shift. What is important? It is not money, and it is not things! They pass away quickly. Bugs can eat them up, thieves can steal them, or they may get rusty. They are not worth a lot of our focus. The heavenly treasures are where we want to focus.

Next, we have to stop worrying! {My number one problem.} Why do we have to stop worrying? Well, it won't help anything, and it hinders our faith. It won't make us any taller. Worrying is a waste of our time.

Now the last thing is to seek first the kingdom of God and His righteousness and then ALL THESE THINGS WILL BE ADDED UNTO YOU!

I have to keep thinking of the life of Jesus on earth. He lived day to day trusting God for His needs and other's needs. He didn't even have cupboards! He lived His life on earth without things. He had what He needed but He had nothing stored on earth. He went from place to place. His focus was on eternal things.

It is Time to Change

It is time for us to change our focus. We need to understand the power of darkness to blind us to the eternal things. We need to realize that this is where the problem lies.

We need to take the blinders off and understand what is really important. Remember what I had learned in AA and AL Anon, that my husband's job was not more important than his sobriety. AA and Al Anon are places where blinders are removed. I learned it was more important for me to let Jim face his consequences and lose his job. That was hard, we had three children and needed money. But the real value was in something invisible, the freedom from denial that kept Jim bound to alcohol.

Darkness blinds the minds of unbelievers, but it can also hinder believers, our minds also need to be set free from blinders or it can hinder our walk with the Lord, it can impair our focus. Our focus needs to be on eternal things.

We also need to understand the power the spirit of the world to blind us and to choke out our faith. The world is getting darker and darker. Those who trust in things like investments and 401k's and even gold and silver are not going to be able to rise above the coming turbulence. Our focus can no longer be on temporal things, it has to be on the eternal. We need to live without the blindness of the kingdom of darkness and have our eyes open to true eternal things of light. Our priorities cannot be on cupboard doors and sheds and floors or on money, money,

money! Those things offer little hope and no eternal security.

If our focus is on Jesus and living for Him, we have eternal hope and security, and our needs will be met.

Chapter Thirteen

The Difference in Masters

Those who choose to serve God and pursue the kingdom of light will have a different experience than those who choose darkness. Both kingdoms are operated totally differently, and each has a different ruler.

Of course, the ruler of the kingdom of light is God, the Father the Son and the Holy Spirit, they operate as One. We will talk about God and how He operates and what you can expect from Him. Those who do not choose to follow God automatically fall under the kingdom of darkness and its ruler is Satan. We will talk about his characteristics also and what to expect from him.

Jesus is God in the flesh. He came out of the invisible realm and dwelt with us. He told Philip His disciple, "He who has seen me has seen the Father." Jesus is the exact image of the unseen God. From Jesus we get our knowledge of God. Jesus on earth represents all of the trinity. They are revealed to us in the person of Jesus.

Love

God is motivated by love. He is the source of love, and He gives love. He created us to be objects of His love. He loved us and He has redeemed us at a very high cost, the blood of Jesus. God's love is immeasurable, it is like an ocean, and it is very deep and vast. Therefore, God's relationship with us is a love relationship. God is the initiator of a loving relationship with us, He loved us first.

God loves us and therefore whenever He deals with us it will be exactly what is best for us. He has the parenting thing down pat. We probably won't always like it or understand the fact that what is best for us isn't always easy, but He sees such a bigger picture than we do. He sees our future a million years from now, and He knows exactly where we need to change.

God loves you and God desires your love in return. But He gives us a free will because love cannot be commanded, that would not be love. Each of us must choose Him for ourselves.

What we can expect from God is love.

Humility and Love

Humility and love go hand in hand. Love can appear very weak in our world. It is not rude, it doesn't demand its own way, and it is not boastful or proud or self-seeking. It suffers long and is kind. It doesn't seem like the most powerful force in existence, but it is.

We had no idea what love looked like until Jesus appeared on the scene. Love appeared in the form of a person, Jesus. And to everyone it looked as though He completely failed in His mission.

Jesus was taken and crucified by a satanically inspired crowd, and He didn't even put up a fight, in fact He didn't even say a word in His own defense. The disciples were expecting Him to become king! They thought when push came to shove, He would take things by force. Instead, He was taken in the night, beat beyond recognition, tried in a mock trial and then crucified. He was spit on, had His beard pulled from His face and a hideous crown of thorns mashed into His brow! Yet, the King of Kings and Lord of Lords uttered not a word. He looked weak and His purpose seemed to those, who were with Him, to have died along with Him.

Jesus did not even fight Satan, at first. He allowed Satan to torment and abuse Him in the underworld and to take Him to the lowest hell. He allowed Satan to make sport of Him in front of the myriads of fallen angels and spirits in the world of darkness.

This was love in action. It looked weak and it looked defeated. Jesus appeared defeated not only to all the earth but also to the entire underworld. But He was not defeated at all; it was love in action, love for mankind, and love for the Father. Jesus allowed Himself to face the lowest hell and then ascended to the highest heaven that He might fill all things. Love acted in utter humility and allowed Himself to be made low, for the objects of His love, for us. This is what God is like!

God is Holy

God is absolutely holy. We have no idea what that is like! We are sinners! God does not tolerate sin. If we were to come to God without the blood of Jesus, His holiness would destroy us. God will abolish wickedness.

We think we are good people because we compare ourselves to someone worse than ourselves, but compared to God, His holiness shows up our filthiness. Our words, our thoughts, our motives and our deeds all come from our own selfishness and very rarely do we actually do something with a pure heart.

God is changing us into His image, but it is a process that takes effort on our part. It takes following the leading of His Holy Spirit down a narrow path, which gets narrower and narrower the further we go. And again, the choice is ours, but the rewards are eternal. We decide our eternal position in Christ by the choices we make on earth. The lower into humility Christ went the higher He reigned. The same is true with us.

So, What Can We Expect from God?

God is so different than I ever imagined Him to be.

He is amazing beyond words. He treats each one of us like we are the only person on earth. He is personal. He is intimate and loving. He is patient with us. He forgives us over and over and He doesn't tire of us.

I get so tired of myself I expect God to do the same. He doesn't.

God will never control us or manipulate us. It is not in His nature. We have the choice to follow Him, in fact we have the choice to go as far in God and as high in His kingdom as WE choose. We make that choice by how we live on this earth.

God is not pushy; in fact, He leads us gently.

I decided when I came to Him that I wanted my life to be about Him and yet... I find I ignore His promptings continually. I still live selfishly, and He gently gets my attention.

Gods Promptings are Gentle

When our oldest daughter, Lonna, was going to Morning Star School, my husband and I drove her back to school from her Christmas break. We decided to stay there for the New Year's conference. It was a dream come true for me. I longed to go to things like that. We have rarely had vacations or traveled. Lonna arranged the hotel for a very low rate. We even planned to travel back to Michigan by way of the southern west tip of Virginia so we could stop and see my prayer partner and best friend Rhonda.

Rhonda and I pray daily by phone and had for many

years. She had been my neighbor when I lived in Florida and we both moved away many years before. For years we stayed in contact by phone as prayer partners except for a few periods when Rhonda could no longer afford a phone. That was very difficult because we rely on each other even though we are a great distance apart. So not only was I going to get to go to a Morning Star Conference, but I was going to see my friend Rhonda on the way home. I was delighted.

While we were at the conference, I spent a lot of time in their bookstore just drooling over the Christian books. I was wishing I could buy every last one of them, and reading as much of them as I could while I browsed. While I was in the store, I noticed a blue leather jacket with the Morning Star logo on it and it was marked way down! There were actually two of them left, one was Jim's size and the other was too small. My husband Jim has a 'thing' for leather coats. I passed it by even though it was extremely cheap because we didn't have extra money to spend.

When I got back in our room, I felt the Lord tell me to go buy the coat for Jim. So, I told Jim about the coat, and he wanted it. I went back down to buy the coat for him but when I got back down to the bookstore the coat was gone! Only the small one was left, the one that was Jim's size was gone! It had sold!

Now I felt confused. Why did the Lord tell me to go buy that coat for Jim and then it was gone? I felt a loss and I felt discouraged. It didn't make sense to me, so I started to pray about it. I didn't just pray, I PRAYED. What was going on? I wanted an answer. It did not make sense to me.

Well, I got an answer, but it was not what I was expecting. Before we had left on our trip, I had a fleeting little thought that I should give Rhonda my keyboard. It was a nice one. Even though I bought it used, it was expensive, and I had made payments on it for a couple of years. It was probably my most prized possession. I loved to play it and would play it for hours. I knew Rhonda had wanted a piano or a keyboard for years, but she was even poorer than I am, and she had never gotten one. Well as soon as that fleeting little thought about giving my keyboard away came into my head, I shot it down. I did not even consider giving my keyboard away.

"The coat was supposed to be for you to give to Jim," the Lord explained to me, "but you disobeyed Me about the keyboard, so you lost that blessing."

"That was You telling me to give up my keyboard, Lord? I thought that was just a bad thought that came into my head."

God never said another word to me about my keyboard, but now I knew how He felt about it.

I was pretty mad at myself. Not only had I missed a blessing but now I had to pay for shipping to send Rhonda my keyboard when I got back home, which I did. I did it because I really do want to please God, more than I wanted to keep my keyboard. I would have never even known that I had missed God if I hadn't PRAYED diligently why I had missed the coat blessing.

God never beat me over the head with His will and

it was up to me whether I obeyed or not, and had I obeyed at first, I would have had a leather coat blessing from it.

God is not pushy! He is loving and kind, but He is leading us out of our own selfishness. Serving God is not easy, but it is wonderful!

God leads us gently.

God is not controlling.

God doesn't cause guilt, or shame, but gentle conviction.

God will not push His will on us, we have to seek it.

God rewards and blesses our obedience.

God always encourages us.

He gives us hope.

He gives us peace.

He operates out of love because it His nature.

God forgives us!

God will never leave us or forsake us.

God protects the weak and the poor and blesses those who bless them

God heals the sick

God humbles Himself to deal with us.

My sister, Carol told me a story that brought tears to my eyes, about the humility of Christ. She and her husband had felt led to return to Bible College for another year even after they had earlier graduated and were working. So, they left their home and returned to Bible College. Money was tight and some of their needs did not get met. Carol felt her faith in God slip because of it. They had stepped out in faith and yet it seemed like God let her down. The Lord dealt with her about it.

He said to her, "I know you feel I let you down."

"It is okay, Lord," Carol replied, "but I wondered why You didn't provide."

"Many times, on earth I operate through people. I had prepared someone to meet your needs, but that person didn't respond."

Then the Lord said something to Carol that made her gasp.

"Will you forgive me?"

"Lord!" Carol cried in amazement, "You would ask me to forgive You? After all You have forgiven me for, and done for me, and You would ask me to forgive You!"

"Yes, I don't want this to come between us."

"Of course, I forgive You Lord! Of course!"

The Lord was so concerned about my sister's faith slipping that He humbled Himself to ask her forgiveness!

That is the kind of God we serve! An awesome caring God that operates in love and humility!

What You Can Expect from Satan

Have you ever read or heard someone's story that has endured torture? I have read many, especially from communist countries and how they treated the Christians. They would beat them and torture them in order to get them to deny their faith. The communists have many tortures they use. Their cruelty is beyond imagination. There are pressure suits and cold cells and needles injected under the fingernails, starvation and beatings.

They are merciless.

This is a picture of the satanic kingdom and how it operates, through fear. Satan uses fear and cruelty to bring his underlings to submission. Those in the satanic realm feed on torture and cruelty, it gives them fiendish delight. Those in his demonic army even despise each other. The only time they can come into agreement is their hatred for God.

That is only the beginning of Satan's characteristics. He uses control, deceit and manipulation. What looks like freedom to those who follow after his, "do whatever you please" mentality really leads to incredible bondage.

There is no freedom in his kingdom. There are no choices. Once he thinks he has you he refuses to let go. Satan has fought for many a soul who repented of their sins near the end of their lives. He fights to keep them. He struggles with God and demands they are legally his. Not that he obeys the laws of God, but he knows God does.

Satan's original sin was pride. He has no humility whatsoever. I believe Satan saw the humility and love of God, and how God is gentle and patient in nature and he saw it as weakness. I believe because of this, in his pride, he actually thought he could overthrow God. Satan looked to himself and not to God; he desired the worship that belongs to God.

Satan also always retaliates and gets revenge. Anytime believers get the better of him they can be ready for a counterattack, which is how Satan operates, he will always seek revenge.

Satan is pushy!

He is controlling and manipulative.

He uses deception and twists the truth.

Everything he says is a lie.

He perverts what God has made.

He is vile and gruesome.

There is no compassion or kindness in him, not a shred.

Satan desires mindless obedience.

He delights in others torment.

He causes confusion and chaos.

Satan oppresses the weak.

Satan is the author of diseases.

One time when I was sitting at church, I felt Satan come down the aisle of the church toward the front. It was a horrible feeling of confusion that surrounded him. It was just as real as if a person were there. I heard him laughing hysterically, as he walked past me. Just then the wife of one of the elders screamed. Her husband had fallen to the floor and was having a heart attack. The whole church began to pray fervently and by the time the ambulance arrived the man was healed and was fine. But I never forgot the horrible feeling of that evil being that walked past me. This is the master, which those who reject Christ choose for themselves.

The One Thing God and Satan Have in Common

The thing that God and Satan both have in common is that they both need our cooperation to operate on planet earth. Without us they are limited to what they can do on earth. Anything we do or say is either helping the kingdom of darkness or the kingdom of light. The will of God and Satan is carried out by human beings on the earth, through words, actions thoughts and deeds.

On a National Level

When people on earth choose God, and they live righteously, Satan has very little power. They enact God's protection over their nation and Satan cannot oppress them. Their land will be blessed and protected by God. They will have victory over their enemies, they will prosper, and they will have safety from natural disasters and plagues and all the things Satan brings with him.

When whole nations reject God, Satan is allowed by them, to come and bring with him the things that he wants to bring on mankind, famine and disasters, wars and bloodshed, plagues and diseases.

God needs the intercessions of His people to intervene in the affairs of earth. It was intercessions of the people of God that turned the tide in World War 2. When God's people neglect to pray, evil will continue. {Remember darkness invades where there is a void of light} We are the body of Christ on the earth, and He operates through us.

The United States and Israel

Israel and the United States are both covenant nations. Both were established to serve God, honor Him and were in covenant with Him. As long as both of these nations kept their end of the covenant they were blessed by God. But as these nations turned to other Gods and forsook the covenant, God's hand of protection was then pulled of these nations. {This is what we in the USA have experienced}

God established through the United States, His will, and that is freedom. Although because of slavery, we received judgement in the form of the Civil War, America faltered but did not fall. We can see in the pattern of these two countries God's blessing and will for a country. It is God's will for people to live in freedom and safety and peace. He wants as much as possible, heaven to come to earth.

Hitler and Communism

Satan has had evil leaders he has raised up throughout history. One of the worst was Hitler. We can see how Hitler was a pre- runner to the anti-christ who is prophesied in the Bible. He was a leader whose desire was to take over the world. We can see how Satan operates from the governments he inspires. Hitler was literally bringing hell to earth through the Third Reich. His concentration camps were hell on earth, the people in them looked like walking skeletons and he was burning people in ovens!

Satan's governments are allowed no freedom. People are reduced to cattle. They are given plain drab clothes to wear and little food. They are driven by merciless guards that will torture and kill anyone who dares not obey. The weak are destroyed. The Jews, God's people, were the main target of his rage.

Communism is very similar. Big Brother is always watching. Christians are tortured, imprisoned and killed. Why? Because they can't be controlled by government, they are controlled by God. Again, the drab lifeless existence, the Chinese Communists dressed the whole nation men and women alike in a universal uniform.

You will see this in every satanically inspired rule or government. Satan wants dumbed down masses. He wants mindless, compliant robotic like submission. It sucks the creativity and individuality out of its people. We see this in communism and Hitler and the Nazi's, and now even in our country there are forces that are trying to move us in this direction. This will be the goal of the anti-christ kingdom, whose beginnings we are starting to see here now.

Fluoride in the drinking water and toothpaste is part of this! Hitler used this toxic chemical to make his millions of subjects in concentration camps more docile and easier to handle. Fluoride affects the brain. So, who's behind it today and why is it in our water and toothpaste????

And how about mercury in our dental work and in

our forced shots, inoculations and flu shots??? Those who refuse these shots are made out to be criminals. I received a letter from my employer that if I did not get a flu shot, I would be fired! I hadn't had the flu in more than twenty years, but I was forced to take a flu shot.

Satan wants his constituents like cattle, dumbed down masses with no creativity at all because he is jealous of our God given creativity, he can't create he only distorts creation.

On the other hand, God encourages creativity and individuality. I hope you don't think we have a uniform in heaven, the white choir robe thing. Everything in heaven has design and beauty including the clothes.

And God doesn't want compliant dumbed down masses, just the opposite. He puts incredible importance on each of us and knows our individual likes and dislikes and encourages our creativity and uniqueness. God and Satan's governments are totally opposite, as different as day and night.

We can see that both of these kingdoms are in operation on earth. Have you ever heard the saying that to those in heaven, earth is the only hell they will ever know and to those in hell, earth is the only heaven they will ever know?

This is a true saying. Both are here. Both kingdoms, light and darkness, are alive and well on earth. Love and hate both exist here, evil and good, truth and deception, the entrance to heaven and the gates to hell. We can choose which one we want to belong to.

Jesus the source and ruler of light or Satan who

dwells in darkness, they both offer something different.

On earth the kingdom of light can look like bondage because we don't live recklessly but carefully and soberly but it leads to incredible freedom.

Satan's kingdom can look like freedom with its free sex and drugs, and anything goes but leads to incredible bondage and slavery. If you choose to follow darkness, you can expect to be treated cruelly and without a shred of kindness. If you choose the kingdom of light you can expect to be loved by an incredible God who created, you to love you. This is the difference between the two masters.

Chapter Fourteen

The Secret Weapon

Our world went through a drastic change at the fall of Adam, the world, mankind and all of creation on the face of the earth. Things were incredibly different back then. The spiritual realm and the physical realm were joined together, in man and on the earth. Earth and nature were also affected, just as man was affected because earth was created for mankind to tend, and it was his home. We have a connection with our world.

Everything was perfect in those days. The earth had a different axis, and it had a layer of ice above the atmosphere which acted as a shield. The weather was perfect. The vegetation grew without sweat and labor. It never rained; a mist would water the earth. Humans did not eat animals and animals did not eat each other. There was no sickness or disease. Communication between man and animals existed. But the greatest thing of all was the relationship that existed between the physical realm and the spiritual realm. It operated together. Man could see God and walk and talk with God. We could eat from spiritual trees that bore spiritual fruit such as the Tree of Life.

The spirit realm seems like a fantasy realm to many in our day and time; some people don't believe it exists. It's a world where things like love and peace are tangible; they have color, smell and taste. It's a world in which humans could operate much like God for they were created in His image. They could speak with thought and travel through time and space with ease. A world we can barely begin to understand, and it's a world that was joined with our physical realm before sin entered the picture.

We are told, before the fall, Adam and Eve were naked and not ashamed; they were clothed in the light of God's glory. This also changes the day Adam fell. Suddenly Adam feels naked, and he is ashamed. It was no longer a supernatural world in which the spiritual and physical flowed as one. We find out what happened to this wonderful world in Genesis 1:15.

Then the Lord God took the man and put him in the Garden of Eden to tend and keep it. And the Lord God commanded the man, saying, "Of every tree of the garden you may freely eat; but of the tee of the knowledge of good and evil you shall not eat, for in the day you eat of it you will surely die."

Death Means Separation from God

This death God was talking about was what death really is. The kind of death that those who never receive Jesus will face, eternal death. We are eternal beings we will never cease to exist. The death God is talking about is separation from Himself. That is what death is, separation from God.

Eternal life is to never be separated from God and eternal death is to be separated from God. This is what Jesus died to give us, an eternity with God. And this is what Adam lost the day he ate of the tree of the knowledge of good and evil.

Adam and Eve and the earth and even the animals living on the earth, all nature experienced a separation from God. We read a little about this in Romans 8:19-22 *For the earnest expectation of the creation eagerly awaits the revealing of the sons of God. For the creation was subject to futility, not willingly, but because of Him who subjected in hope; because the creation itself also will be delivered from the bondage of corruption into glorious liberty of the children of God. For we know that the whole of creation groans and labors with the birth pangs together until now.*

Creation actually suffered the fall, with man. We see a different creation now since the fall. We have the natural which is defiled through sin, without the spiritual. Death is everywhere now. Corruption has entered the picture and the supernatural is cut off. Decay and disease are now a part of creation. These things were not here before. Now we have thorns and thistles, bees that sting, mold and mildew rust and corruption. The weather is no longer perfect, we have storms and earthquakes, droughts and floods. And the vital part of everything, the spiritual, has been cut off.

Creation has changed; it was something more. This reminds me of the many, many testimonies I have read of heaven, which is a passion of mine and has been my entire life. Those who visit heaven always comment on nature there. They see wild animals like lions which are completely tame. The flowers and grass and trees are more beautiful and perfect than those on earth. They have qualities earthly creation doesn't have. They seem to be worshipping the Lord. Some have said it actually seems that the flowers turn to look as the Lord passes them by and that there is a sound of worship coming off of them. It seems the plants and trees actually worship God.

Could there be more to nature than we realize? Yes!

I once heard a speaker who said that plants respond to music and what goes on around them, even words spoken to them. This was the way things were before the fall.

{And I would even like to speculate about the big global warming issue. Our earth and the nature we live with, loathe sin. Sin is causing our earth's problems! The earth is quaking and shaking. The weather has become violent and unpredictable, and nature is violently opposing the stench of mankind's sin!!!!! That is what is causing the problems on the earth. And they are only going to get worse because man is getting increasingly wicked.}

Mankind and creation on earth died the day Adam and Eve ate from the knowledge of good and evil, we died spiritually, we became separated from God. The spiritual realm was totally rent from the physical realm. Let's talk about how this affects mankind, me and you.

We are separated from God now and we know longer can access the spiritual realm or God. We are incredibly dead in that area. Our bodies are still alive, but scripture calls them a body of death.

Wretched man that I am! Who shall deliver me from the body of this death? Romans 7:24

We suffered death in three realms that day, our bodies our souls and our spirits. We are now a fallen creature and subject to Satan, in these three areas. Our bodies now feel pain and sickness. Our emotional realm can also feel pain and many other negative emotions such as hatred, envy, anger and lust. Our spirits have also been rendered worthless we can no longer communicate with God. We are stuck in a world without contact with God, the spirit realm is unapproachable.

There is now a thick black veil separating our world from that world, a world we were meant to be a part of. We were created to dwell in both realms simultaneously. The physical realm is caught in death. We now experience the clutch of darkness. We do not know how to activate or engage the realm of God. We are separated from God. The knowledge of God soon begins to fade as the spirit of darkness convinces mankind that this earthly life is all there is.

Born Again

Jesus came to redeem this situation. But what does that mean? Our earth is still in the clutches of death. Sin and corruption still plague the earth and things don't look that much different.

What Jesus did for us is very real; it is very real in the spirit realm, the real world. A change has been made but what is that change?

What happens to us when we become born again? Our spirit becomes alive again! We are now reattached to God in our spirit. In this area we take on the righteousness in Christ and our spirit becomes joined with His.

But we still have two areas that are still in darkness, our souls and our bodies. Our soul needs to be renewed and reprogrammed. We are still locked into this physical realm by our minds and bodies. Our bodies also age, get sick and die.

The day is coming when are bodies will be resurrected like Jesus body was, we have that promise. But until that day we live in a body tied to the physical realm that cannot access the spiritual world. And the earth and creation are still waiting for their redemption. The day when the sons of God are revealed. Our redemption has come but it is in the spirit realm, and it still needs to be brought into the physical realm.

The Secret Weapon

Wouldn't it be nice if we had something that could help us cross over to that realm, the invisible world of the spirit? Something tangible in the physical realm that we could see and touch but something that would help us in another realm, a supernatural object, half physical, half spiritual, something, a tool to reconnect us. To help us activate light and life back into our physical realm.

We have that something!

We have that miraculous spiritual something. It is sitting on our shelves. It contains a power that can transform us and heal us. It contains a power so great that Satan fears it. It can be used in both realms, seen in both realms and experienced in both realms although it looks different in each.

What is it?

It is the Bible.

In one world it appears as an antiquated book, in the other, a powerful sword with a life of its own.

The Bible is so supernatural that it boggles the mind. It is a tangible physical book, paper and ink. You can pick it up and hold it is real, natural physical. And yet it is spiritual; it is alive, living and active. It is a sword that cuts through the thick veil of darkness and accesses the realm of light, the eternal realm of God. It dispels darkness and terrifies devils.

It is a portal; we pick up a book in the natural; we pick up a sword in the spirit. It is the living spoken word of God, the same power that created the universe, but it is also something each and every person can have. Do we value this powerful weapon, this supernatural tool that can access both realms?

The Most Amazing Book

The Bible is supernatural, alright! The Bible tells us the beginning of the world and the Bible tells us the ending of this world. It tells us the ending from the beginning. It predicts the future, and it informs us of the past.

It is a most amazing book.

The Bible predicted, to the day, when Jesus would enter Jerusalem riding on a donkey. It told us about Jesus long before He was born.

It tells us what the end of days will be like and even the final judgement when we stand before God to be judged.

The Bible was written over a 1600-year period by approximately forty writers and yet it flows together perfectly.

The Bible is a most holy book. People have been healed reading its words. I have. People have received hope in their darkest hour reading it, I have. People have received eternal life reading the words of the Bible. It is also a powerful weapon against our enemies.

I have used it when the powers of darkness have surrounded me, and it delivered me.

Many soldiers in many battles have clung to the words of the Bible as they faced their enemies in battle.

The words of the Bible gave them courage, protected them, and gave them great hope.

The words of the Bible are clung to, by those who need help. Many times, the words of the Bible are the last thing on the lips of the dying.

We who have just a glimpse of its power rise up early to read it and keep it running throughout our minds throughout the day, we live by it.

We will never uncover the secret riches in the Bible there are so many of them. Its truths run deeper than the human mind can comprehend. They contain layer after layer of treasure and hidden meaning that only the diligent can unveil.

This has happened to me. The words have literally come alive as I have read them and as I have caught them and latched on. They have become faith in my heart for miracles, for provision, for strength, hope and victory.

The Bible is also science and history, and it is wisdom and truth. It is a telescope far into the future and takes us back to the day of creation, and even before.

It has also given me my dearest of friends, my family. They have become my mentors; their names are Noah and Abraham, Joseph and Moses, Joshua and Daniel and David and Jonah. Their lives from the Bible have cleared the path before me and they from heaven cheer me on daily to run after them and join them. But how would I have known them if I had not read their stories in the greatest book ever written, the Bible.

The Bible is a portal, it takes us up to heaven to receive from God. We boldly access the Throne of Grace and receive from Him, the provisions the Bible clearly states we have received, through the sacrificed lamb, Jesus. The Bible makes this possible.

The Bible even contains secret codes embedded in the original texts. Some who have studied these codes have found every event in history embedded in Bible codes. Some think that every person on earth may possibly be embedded in Bible codes. They have found myriads of historic events, from the holocaust to the landing on the moon from Watergate to the death of Princess Diana. All have been found encrypted in the Bible. The Bible is a puzzle to be unfolded.

The Bible is the all-time best seller and has been translated into 531 languages. There is no other book like the Bible. Men have given their lives to translate this book into other languages, others have risked prison to smuggle it into communist countries which outlaw it. Others have been imprisoned for merely owning or reading it.

The powers of darkness have tried to banish it to no avail. They have convinced men its fantasy and tried to pass it off as nonsense. Why? Because Satan and all his cohorts fear this powerful weapon which has been placed into our realm disguised as a mere book. It is a mighty weapon of light to use against darkness!

Men have died for this book. They lay down their

lives just to own it. They have died rather than renounce it. Why? Because it is like no other book. Its words are eternal.

The grass withers, the flower fades, but the word of our God endures forever. Isaiah 40:8

For those of us who belong to the Kingdom of Light, we have something from home, something real and tangible. We have something that will last forever. Something that contains God's power. Something that can change us. Something that can heal us. Something that we can pick up and activate and defeat our enemies. Most of us do not realize its power.

It's been called a double-edged sword.

It has been declared eternal.

It has been called a light unto our pathway and a lamp for our feet.

It's been called sweeter than honey, more to be desired than gold.

It causes us to prosper and succeed.

It will never come back void.

It renews our minds.

It contains the answers for life, the secrets of life and death.

It is more than just words on a page, it is living and active and powerful!

It is physical and it is spiritual, it is our secret weapon.

Do good to me that, your servant, so I can live Open my eyes to see the miracles in your teachings Psalms 119:17-18

Lord, your word is everlasting; it continues forever in heaven Psalms 119:89

Chapter Fifteen

Angels and Demons

How unreal it seems that there is an invisible world operating all around us. Unseen spirits are in the very room we are in and yet we are oblivious to their activities. But their activities affect us, and it is important business. We need to know and understand some things about this invisible world and how we can cooperate in it.

Angels are here for us. They minister to us, they protect us, and they are working along with us. They are assigned to us by God, some even from our birth. They are constantly working around us. But they can't live our lives for us; we have to do that for ourselves.

What do I mean by that? I mean your angels can greatly help you in your life and your walk with God or their hands can be tied. The choice is yours. Angels are constantly working even in the lives of those who are unsaved. They work to bring them about to the point of making the choice to serve God. If they do not choose the Lord, the angels will start all over again. But the choice is still ours.

And for those of us who are saved, if we walk in faith and peace our angels are free to minister to us. But if we walk in anger, depression and bitterness we still open the door to the demonic.

The more we walk in light; the more angelic activity will be present in our lives because we will attract the angelic activity. The more we walk in darkness; the more demonic activity will be present in our lives because we will attract the demonic.

Remember what we learned in chapter 9, that our thoughts and attitudes are tangible in the spirit realm. They either put out light color and smell that is sweet and beautiful or dinghy and foul, we are either attracting light or darkness.

Cooperating with Angels

We have to learn to walk in light and to cooperate with angels or in other words cooperate with God who always wants what is best for us.

Angels aren't a magic trick to help us get what we want, like a lucky charm. They will not help you stay selfish and spoiled and do your bidding like Aladdin's magic lamp. If what we want is to live completely for the kingdom of

God, they will help, but we still have the responsibility to do our part. We have to grow up and put forth effort.

Now, having said that, I have received great help and encouragement from angels. I told in my book, *The Impossible Marriage,* how my angel Charlie helped me greatly in my marriage. In fact, I believe Charlie is an angel assigned to our marriage.

My husband, Jim and I were going through such a difficult period in our marriage I didn't think I would survive. We were fighting constantly about a situation we were at odds about.

My prayer partner, Rhonda was praying for me and told me there was an angel named Charlie in my house. She said he had curly blonde hair and was wearing a sailor cap, and he was full of laughter. She explained that when Jim and I were fighting, I was to get quiet and listen for Charlie's laughter and he would fill me with joy.

I had a choice; I could think that was crazy and keep being miserable or I could obey and in the middle of turmoil get quiet and listen for Charlie.

I tried it. Jim and I were in a heated argument, and I listened. I heard beautiful tinkley laughter. Not with my physical ears, with my spiritual ears. Charlie's laughter would fill me with joy, and I would begin laughing too. Then my husband Jim would begin laughing. It changed our marriage.

What Charlie was doing by laughing was getting my eyes off of strife and onto the joy of the Lord! He was getting me to switch channels, from darkness to light. He helped me! I still had to do it each time, but he helped me!

I actually could not have done it without him. I learned to cooperate with my angel.

I got another little glimpse of the importance of cooperating with angels another time. My husband was suffering with a real bout of depression. He was shut up in the bedroom and was inconsolable. This happens every so often. This particular time my daughter, Joy was over, and she could see Jim's angel. {She sees angels on a regular basis.} He was pacing back and forth in front of Jim's bedroom door. He wanted to help Jim, but he couldn't. He wanted Jim to worship with him. {Jim normally loves to worship} Jim was too wrapped up in the darkness.

I realized something that day as that angel was pacing so. I realized that we have to cooperate with them. They can help us when we choose to walk in light, but if we choose darkness their hands are tied.

Another time I had a lesson about cooperating with angels. It was during a hurricane. It was heading toward Florida and directly toward the city where my mother lives. It was a category four. My prayer buddies, my sister and my daughter and I spent a lot of time in prayer, not only for my mother but for those who would be affected by the hurricane.

In the middle of the night, the same night of the hurricane, my bedroom filled with angels. I could sense them in the room, but I did not know why they were there. I wondered if they had come from protecting my mother, I didn't know. I concluded maybe they had just come to let me know the job was done. The next time my prayer buddies and I gathered for prayer I found out. My daughter, Joy is much more sensitive to the spirit realm than I am. As we were praying, she saw the angels that had come into my room that night. They told her why they had come. They needed you to intercede so they could help more people. I realized I hadn't responded correctly. Now when I wake up and sense angels in my room, I pray.

Angels Don't Hide Their Emotions

I also noticed how angels do not cover their emotions like we do. I like this. They are very transparent with their emotions. I notice when they laugh, they really laugh loudly. When they are upset, they show that too. They are beautiful beings without sin, that love the Lord and they don't have the superficiality we humans do. They embrace their own personalities and emotions shamelessly, something that is very foreign to me. Jim's angel was distressed for Jim, and he showed it, by animatedly pacing back and forth in front of Jim's door.

Face to Face with an Angel

That same day Joy saw Jim's angel pacing, I was jealous that I couldn't see the angels like Joy could. I longed to see in the spirit as well as she could. Joy said, "Mom just look in the spirit, there are angels here. Just look!"

I strained to look in the spirit. I could sort of see an angel. Things looked blurry just like when my glasses are off, but I could sort of see an angel. Then the angel I was straining to see put his face right up to my face so I could see him perfectly. Our faces were about an inch apart. He had the most wonderful grin on his face, as he stuck his face up to my face; I still smile when I think of it! In fact, I am smiling writing about it. It was an infectious smile, and he had a twinkle in his eye. Angel's emotions are so transparent I knew what he was thinking; he was thinking, "You want to see me! Here see me!" But what surprised me the most was that his facial features were almost identical to Joy's. I realized he was Joy's guardian angel.

He certainly surprised me! I had peeked into his realm, and he had peeked back. But what surprised me the most was what a delightful sense of humor he had and how real he was.

Joy's Experiences with Angels

My daughter Joy has had many experiences with angels that have helped her immensely. One time was back when she was sixteen Joy was going through an especially difficult time. She had gone through rejection from a church leader who had disagreed on a sermon she had taught, and he banned her from ministry. Although this was a difficult lesson it was an important one. She was learning the difference between pleasing men and pleasing God. But that is only in hindsight she realized this; at the time she was devastated.

Joy went and stayed with her brother who was in

Bible College at the time. She spent many hours in the prayer chapel there. This particular experience she had was while she was praying in the in the prayer chapel.

Joy was feeling like a failure, and she opened up her heart to the Lord.

"Lord, I want to be a Christian," she earnestly prayed thinking she somehow failed the Lord by being banned from ministry and upsetting the pastor, "but I just don't know how, it is too hard!"

Suddenly she was interrupted. The voice was very clear but not loud, in fact the interruption was done politely, very politely. "Excuse me, I don't mean to interrupt, but I am here to help."

Joy was in the presence of an angel. He introduced himself as Barnabas. He had curly brown hair, and he was dressed in a purple robe with a matching purple band around his head. After introducing himself, Barnabas told Joy, "I want to show you something."

Joy got up and followed Barnabas leaving her body behind in prayer. He led Joy into a hallway. It was beautiful beyond words. The ceilings were high, and the walls and pillars were made of a cream color marble that had gold and white flecks in it. The room was softly lit, and beautiful chandeliers hung from the ceiling. The room was long and narrow and appeared to be a gallery, like an art museum.

Barnabas led Joy to the first picture in the gallery; it was of a very small little girl coming to a cross. As Joy looked at the picture it came to life and Joy watched in amazement. Suddenly Joy cried out, "That's me!" The picture was of Joy coming to the Lord, she was very young.

This art gallery was a gallery of Joy's life!

The next picture in the gallery was Joy getting baptized. Joy stopped in front of it and watched the scene, reliving it as she watched.

{I will always remember that day she was baptized. She was only four years old, and she was determined to be baptized, she wouldn't take no for answer. I was a little upset I did not have my camera with me because it was such a beautiful moment. Tears came to my eyes, and I gasped for breath, as my beautiful, tiny girl came up out of the water. I felt God in such a powerful way; I wanted to hold onto that moment forever. Little did I realize it had been painted in this beautiful gallery of Joy's life.}

As Joy went to each picture, she relived the milestones in her life between her and the Lord. Each was recorded on canvas, and each came to life as she would stop and look at the portraits of her life.

Barnabas explained to her, "Each piece of art is a moment you have had with the Lord. This is a hall of moments." Barnabas looked at Joy and smiled and with a twinkle in his eyes he added, "Precious moments."

Joy realized how ridiculous her desperate prayer had been, she was living a Christian life. It wasn't about church and pleasing her pastor, it was about her moments she was living with the Lord.

As they continued down the hall Joy saw a radiant white cloud ahead. The hall ahead was her future and there were angels waiting, ready to continue to paint the scenes to come. As Joy saw the cloud of glory down the hall ahead of them Barnabas explained to her there was great glory ahead in her life and her future was very bright.

Barnabas explained to Joy, "The glory cloud is the Lord's love. Don't be distracted by the glory cloud. It will also cause others to be attracted to you. Don't let this cloud distract you from the Lord and His love itself."

Then Joy explained to Barnabas that every time she would try to pray or read her Bible; she would get distracted. Barnabas led Joy to a desk with an open Bible. It was open to Isaiah 45. Barnabas told Joy to start there, at Isaiah 45.

Later that day Joy rushed back home to read her Bible. As she read Isaiah 45 the chapter came alive to her as the Holy Spirit spoke to her through it. For weeks after this experience her prayer and Bible study came easy to her and she was able to spend many hours a day in prayer and Bible study.

Barnabas was immediately sent to Joy in answer to her prayer that she had prayed to the Lord. In fact, while she was still praying Barnabas was there, in answer to prayer for help.

Joy has learned to recognize and cooperate with the angels assigned to help her, but God is no respecter of persons He has millions and millions of angels, and they are ministering to you also.

Another time Joy met an angel named William. This was during a time when Joy was in Morningstar Prophetic School. She started when she was still only seventeen. Morningstar is a powerful school of ministry, which doesn't go unnoticed by the powers of darkness. The witches in the area would pray against the students. Joy was having trouble at night during this time and demons would appear in her room at night and sometimes also warlocks. Joy, being very sensitive to the spirit realm, would see them in her room and it would scare her.

It was one of these nights when she met William. She found out William was a camper angel. Camper angels, she learned, camp around the believers to protect them. They build a fire and sit around it at night.

"Do you want to see something?" William asked Joy. He led Joy to the fire burning in her room and then William pulled a sword out of the fire. As he pointed the sword, fire shot forth from it for a great distance. As William was showing Joy the sword, he heard something. A demon jumped up and immediately William zapped it with the sword of fire. It was immediately gone.

"That was only a scarecrow." William explained to Joy. "Spirits of fear are nothing, they are only shadows, there is nothing to them."

From that time on, Joy was no longer afraid at night, knowing William was camping around his fire in her room at night.

Another angel Joy became aware of, that same night, was Bernard. He was a window washer angel. He washes the windows of the soul. Joy remembered the scripture in Revelation 3:18, *I counsel you to buy from Me gold refined in the fire, that you may be rich; and white garments that you may be clothed, that the shame of your nakedness may not be revealed; and anoint your eyes with eye salve that you may see.*

As she was looking at Bernard, she was squirted in the eye. Bernard was doing his spiritual work on her.

Lately Joy is still seeing angels. She just saw some on New Year's Day. The angel she saw introduced himself as Geishar. He was a waiter angel. He was delivering bread, and he gave some to Joy. She said the bread had a purifying effect. He and other waiter angels, Joy met two more, are bringing their bread to those who spend intimate time with the Lord this year. They are on a special mission. They are serving bread and bonding together with the Lord those who make time to be intimate with Him.

Angels are one of the many ways that God shows His love for us. He reaches out to us in love through sending His servants the angels. They reflect Him to us.

Demons

I don't want to say a whole lot about demons because I'd rather talk about angels except to say this. Demons are constantly looking to oppress us, and they are doing this by looking for a legal right to oppress you. Everything in the spirit realm is done by a legal system.

When we are dealing with demons, we do not pray and ask God to remove demons we command them to leave.

I have noticed this when dealing with demons; many times, they will argue and refuse to leave claiming they have a legal right to be there. It may be the person who sinned or opened the door to the demonic or could have even been a parent or some other relative. The way to deal with demons that have a legal right to be there is through repentance and applying the blood of Jesus. Sometimes in praying for others, we have repented for another person and then applied the blood of Jesus, and then we can get rid of the demons.

If you have ever played Euchre, and you understand trump, repentance and the blood of Jesus trumps everything in the spirit realm!

Repentance and the blood of Jesus wash us clean! When we are standing in prayer at the court of the Lord and Satan is accusing us day and night of our sins and demanding his rights, {revelation 12:10} repentance and the blood of Jesus will silence him every time, that's trump.

The best way to stay free of the demonic is not to give the devil any legal rights; this requires diligence, especially with our mouths. *Ephesians 4:27* tells us not to give any place to the devil or some versions say no foothold.

James 4:7 Resist the devil and he will flee from you.

The best way to have the angelic working in your life is to give them a godly foothold. Praying, worshipping, and speaking God's word can activate angels and give them freedom to operate in your life. Living our lives in the light, gives God's angels a foothold.

There is a lot of activity in the invisible realm of the spirit. Whether we realize it or not the spirit realm is going on all around us. Angels and demons are seeking to operate in our lives. We want to cooperate with the angels, and we do not want to give the devil any footholds. We can also begin to use our spiritual eyes to see in that realm, and maybe even begin to see our angels.

If you're having trouble seeing, just ask for Bernard to come and wash your windows!!!

Chapter Sixteen

Day and Night

You are all sons of the light and sons of the day. We are not of the night nor of the darkness. Therefore, let us not sleep as others do, but let us watch and be sober. For those who sleep, sleep at night, and those who get drunk are drunk at night. But let us who are of the day be sober, putting on the breastplate of faith and love, and as a helmet the hope of salvation.   *1 Thessalonians 5:5-8*

There are those that are living their lives as if in a slumber. They have been lulled into a false sense of security like drunkenness. They are living their lives in darkness. The Bible uses words like sleeping and drunkenness to describe the children of the night.

Then the Bible speaks of sons of the light and of the day. We are told not to sleep; we are to be awake. The Bible warns us who are living for the kingdom of light to remain sober and to watch. We live our lives opposite of the night. We must be alert and watchful, we cannot be lulled to sleep. What are we watching for?

We are told in 1Peter 5:8 *Be sober, be vigilant; because your adversary the devil walks about like a roaring lion, seeking whom he may devour.*

The word vigilant means keeping careful watch for possible difficulties. We need to be vigilant because our adversary seeks to destroy us. We have an enemy whether we like it or not.

We get even more cautionary words in Ephesians 5:14-16 *Therefore He says; "Awake, you who sleep, Arise from the dead and Christ will give you light." See then that you walk circumspectly, not as fools but as wise, redeeming the time because the days are evil.*

Circumspectly means carefully. We are told we are living in days that are evil. We are living in a world covered in a thick cloud of darkness made up of fear and depression, which is getting thicker and darker all the time. But we are not of the darkness or the night we are of the day. We need to stay living in the light, even though we are in this dark, dark world. This takes watchfulness on our parts, watchfulness, carefulness and sobriety.

I really get this illustration of drunk and sober because my husband Jim has struggled with alcoholism our whole marriage. The thing that is so prevalent about being drunk is you don't know what is going on! Everything is falling apart all around you and you don't know it! Your mind has been influenced by alcohol and you see the world through a foggy haze. You are not in control, and you are out of reality. Another force is in control that leads you down, down, down.

My husband in his drinking days, told me that he would find himself in unusual places. Once he woke up in the morning on a park bench. He didn't know how he got there, and he had to find his way home. Then another time he fell down coming home. Jim told me that story of how he had fallen in a ditch one dark night on his way home and was too drunk to get up. He said God sent him a big black angel to help him. He was lying there helpless when he heard singing. Then a loving old black man, as jolly as can be, came and looked down and said, "Well, what are you doing down there?" He pulled Jim out and helped him on his way. Jim was sure he was an angel.

Jim would come home black and blue, severely beaten up and not even remember what happened! This happened several times. Once it was such a shock to Jim when he woke up with a purple face, the very next day he checked into the detox center.

One night my husband was trying to wander home drunk, and he was going in the wrong direction. Our dog, Sam, who was so loyal to him, had followed him out. Jim told me Sam was trying to get him turned around, but he was sure he was going in the right direction. Sam would lie down in front of him and was trying everything he could think of to get Jim home. Finally, after going miles in the wrong direction Jim wised up and followed Sam home.

Similarly, those who live in darkness, spiritually, wander. They cannot find their way. They are often going in the wrong direction, and they are frequently getting beat up, and sometimes they fall into a ditch, and they cannot get up. Many try to turn them around, but they are determined they know where they are going.

I found a tool much later in our marriage that I wish I had known about earlier. I videotaped my husband while he was drunk and showed him the next day. It literally woke him up. He was appalled and immediately went to our doctor and asked to be put on Antabuse. Many different times it would take a shock to wake Jim up and get him back on track to get sober.

If we begin to fall asleep spiritually the Lord will have to send us a shock to get us back on track. The problem with sleeping spiritually is that we miss what God wants to do in our lives. Instead of sleeping away our lives in a state of spiritual drunkenness, we should be continually seeking God and finding out for ourselves what His will for us is; in order to do that we need to become alert and sober, spiritually.

God had to just recently wake me up from a complacent attitude. My husband and I were talking about the dangers in our society and our country such as Isis. I flippantly said, "I'm not afraid of Isis."

That night I had a dream. In the dream I was standing on the edge of our city and looking off to the east. These ominous dark funnel clouds began touching down and out of them came these giants and they began marching across the land. They were larger than life and coming fast. They were horrible and fearsome. I ran to escape but it was too late, they were coming, and I couldn't escape. So, I ran looking for a hiding place because I was terrified!!!!! I woke up shaking. I realized I was not ready at all for what is coming. I was just being naive about the danger on our horizon.

I called my daughter and my sister and told them the dream. I told them I was not prepared for what was coming. They both agreed that neither were they and we have started to meet weekly to pray for a couple hours. The express purpose of our prayers is for ourselves and our families to be ready for what is coming to this nation. It took a dream to wake me up!

To be children of the day we have to be alert and sober! We need to be watching spiritually and not lulled into a false sense of security. How can we do this? Let's read a little further in Ephesians.

Therefore, do not be unwise, but understand what the will of the Lord is. And do not be drunk with wine, in which is dissipation; but be filled with the Spirit, speaking to one another in psalms and hymns and spiritual songs, singing and making melody in your heart to the Lord, giving thanks always for all things to God the Father in the name of the Lord Jesus Christ, submitting to one another in the fear of God. Ephesians 5:17-21

It takes work to be awake. It takes discipline, diligence, watchfulness, soberness and prayerfulness.

We need to stay filled with the Holy Spirit. We need to help each other stay built up in the faith. We need to be thankful and submissive.

We also need to stay sober and alert to be ready for the coming of the Lord in our lives. And when I say this, it is more than just the return of the Lord. Not everyone will be alive on the day the Lord returns but everyone's life will end at some point. They will have to give an account of their life to the Lord. Because our life could end at any moment, we need to stay alert. Jesus spoke of staying ready.

But of that day and hour no one knows, not even the angels of heaven, but My Father only. But as the days of Noah were, so also will the Son of Man be. For as the days before the flood, they were eating and drinking, marrying and giving in marriage, until the day that Noah entered the ark, and did not know until the flood came and took them all away, so also will the coming of the Son of man be. Then two men will be in the field: one will be taken and the other left. Two women will be grinding at the mill: one will be taken and the other left. Watch therefore, for you do not know what hour your Lord is coming. But know this, that if the master of the house had known what hour the thief would come, he would have watched and not allowed his house to be broken into. Therefore, you also be ready, for the Son of man is coming at an hour you do not expect.

Matthew 24:36-44

Jesus told us in this passage to WATCH and to BE READY. This is a way of life for those who live in the kingdom of light. We are children of the light and children of the day. The characteristics are then to live carefully. The characteristics of those who are of the night are that they are asleep, and they are drunk, and they are careless. They need to be woken up before it is too late.

But the end of all things is at hand; therefore, be serious and watchful in your prayers. 1Peter 4:7

Therefore we must give more earnest heed to the things we have heard lest we drift away Hebrews 2:1

"Be watchful and strengthen the things which remain, that are ready to die, for I have not found your works to be perfect before God. Remember therefore how you have received and heard; hold fast and repent. Therefore, if you will not watch, I will come upon you as a thief, and you will not know what hour I will come upon you. Revelation3:2-3

Behold I am coming as a thief. Blessed is he who watches and keeps his garments, lest he walk naked and they see his shame. Revelation 16:7

And so we have the prophetic word confirmed, which you do well to heed as a light that shines in a dark place, until the day dawns and the morning star rises in your hearts. 2 Peter1:19

Chapter Seventeen

Choices

For God so loved the world that He gave his only begotten Son, that whosoever believes in Him should not perish but have everlasting life. For God did not send his Son into the world to condemn the world, but that the world through Him might be saved. He who believes in Him is not condemned; but he who does not believe is condemned already, because he has not believed in the name of the only begotten Son of God. And this is the condemnation, that light has come into world, and men loved darkness rather than the light, because their deeds were evil. For everyone who does evil hates the light, lest his deeds should be exposed. But he who does the truth comes to the light that his deeds may be clearly seen that they are done in God." John 3:16-21

When God placed Adam in the Garden of Eden with his wife, Eve, He gave them a choice. The choice was to obey Him. God put the Tree of Life in the Garden, but He also put the tree of the knowledge of Good and Evil. These were in the days when the spirit realm and the physical realm were connected. These trees had spiritual qualities, the Tree of Life causes eternal life and of the Tree of the Knowledge of Good and Evil they were strictly forbidden to eat. In fact, they were told on the day they ate of it they would surely die!

They died because they were separated from God at that point. Real death, eternal death is actually separation from God, as we discussed in a previous chapter. We will never cease to exist, so death is not to cease existing, there is no such thing. Death is to be separated from God.

The point is God gave Adam and Eve a choice, the choice to choose their own destiny. They had the choice to follow God or to turn away in disobedience. The two trees were the choice. When Adam and Eve disobeyed and ate from the tree God had forbidden them to eat from, death came immediately to Adam to the earth and to everything on the earth. Darkness gained a huge victory.

Our choice, today, looks a little different than Adam's. We are born into a fallen world and in a fallen state. It is our normal. We have the choice to choose life through Jesus Christ. We have the choice to go against the normal and choose obedience and a narrow path following Christ, to switch kingdoms, from the kingdom of darkness to the kingdom of light.

It is not always very easy. We are switching from the seen to the unseen, from the visible to the invisible. We are giving up everything we can see and everything we know, to follow something we can only dimly see with eyes of our spirit, which can often seem like a fairy tale. Many will think we are crazy and at times we wonder if they are correct. Everything in this new kingdom is backwards from everything we have never known. We give instead of take. When others do us harm, we act rather strangely. When they slap us on one cheek, we turn the other one to them. When they hate us and cheat us, we bless them and pray for them. We forgive instead of getting even.

Our choice now is to follow Jesus, a man who lived and died two thousand years ago. The world, those who choose to stay in darkness, they think we are crazy. They have made up some names to describe what they think of us, "religious nuts" "Jesus freaks" "holy rollers". They don't understand us.

But the real truth is Jesus is more than just a man who lived and died two thousand years ago. He is the light, the eternal light, the King of Light, who came into a dark world, to free us. We, who are wrapped in chains of darkness and eternally doomed and He offers us a way to freedom. The choice is ours. God has given us a free will to choose Him. Each and every day we make choices that affect our lives. We are still choosing between the Tree of

Life and the Tree of the Knowledge of Good and Evil. The Tree of Life is the choice to follow God and live in obedience to Him. It is the way of fellowship with God and walking in His Garden. The Tree of Life is Jesus, and we take it by faith. This is life to us, and freedom and we still have to choose this tree on a daily basis.

The Tree of the Knowledge of Good and Evil is the opposite of the Tree of Life. We seek to be good on our terms and we focus on ourselves. This tree is death. We can eat of it and follow our own way instead of God's. The fruit of this tree gives a false sense of security of trusting in our own righteousness. We follow our own ways and reject God's.

This is the fruit eaten by those who belong to Babylon. Remember our two cities on the earth, Babylon and Jerusalem. These are the two kingdoms that still exist today. They are the Kingdom of Light and the kingdom of darkness. They are also the two kingdoms that war within us. The choice between these two kingdoms and these two trees are still just as alive and well on earth today as they ever were.

The knowledge of good and evil can be very deceptive because it looks good. We do good works to justify ourselves. We try to earn our way to heaven with wonderful works. Now we are proud, and we feel we are good, and our own righteousness will get us to heaven. But we are still focused on ourselves and not on God. Our own good works can never save us they only prove to lead us further from God and further from the truth. This is eating from the wrong tree. Our own reasoning will always lead us to do the opposite of God's will.

The only true righteousness is coming into agreement with God. As Abraham humbled himself and walked in obedience to God, he became righteous through faith. This is true righteousness, taking up our cross and in humility following Christ, not our own way, no matter how righteous we think our own way is. This is eating from the Tree of Life.

We are continually faced with the choice between kingdoms, between trees, between light and darkness. The choice is ours.

Chapter Eighteen

You are the Light of the World

Arise, Shine; For your light has come! And the glory of the Lord is risen upon you. For behold, the darkness shall cover the earth, And deep darkness shall cover the people, But the Lord will arise over you, And His glory shall be seen upon you. Isaiah 60:1-2

The world has always been a mixture of light and darkness. We have good people and not so good people. There are beautiful places and there are slums. There is love and there is hate. There are soft little bunnies and there are venomous snakes, sunshiny days or tornadoes.

We see a world that offers both good and evil, light and darkness. Everything that is wonderful is here and things that are very terrible. We have all experienced both. Some think the world is a wonderful place and others think it is a living hell, and both are correct.

As we draw closer to the end of the age, things are beginning to come to a head. Seeds that have been planted from the beginning of time are coming into fruition. The kingdom of God and the kingdom of the devil are both drawing apart and becoming more pronounced. The time is now here that there will be no more grey areas; it will be white or black. Those who are light are becoming brighter; those who are in darkness are in gross darkness.

The day will come when God will permanently get rid of the darkness. He will separate the light and darkness forever. They will never dwell together again.

Heaven and Hell

Heaven and hell are like two magnetic poles, one positive and one negative. Depending on how a person is charged, is what will determine which pole they will automatically be pulled to when their spirit leaves their body at the end of their life.

Those who have filled their selves with the light of Christ are positively charged, there is a constant pull heavenward on their lives and after they die. They will be pulled upward to their eternal home. Likewise, those who have never come to the light of Jesus and have filled their life with darkness have become negatively charged and will feel the tug of hell upon their souls. Sometimes people even feel this before they die. In their last moments on earth people will begin to experience either heaven or hell depending on what pole they are being attracted to.

Many people see their deeds as good but have rejected Christ. They are in deception. True holiness is so far from human goodness, that human goodness is dark in comparison. We only have hope through the light of Christ.

Because we are used to good and evil in the same place, we have no idea of just how good heaven is, it is so much better than we can possibly imagine. And likewise, hell is so much worse than the mind can comprehend. When we pull the two away from each other we have extreme good and extreme evil.

Heaven is a place where only good exists. God is the source of all light, of all love of all peace, joy and goodness. The closer we get to the source, the stronger these things become until it is more than we can contain. We don't even understand this kind of delight and fulfillment. Those who have seen heaven and come back are at a loss for words to try to tell us, they try but words fail them. No one that has ever gotten a glimpse of heaven has wanted to return to this lesser life.

In heaven every desire of every person is met. God knows our desires way more than we do ourselves! Can you imagine your delight? Those secret desires you have always wished or imagined are your loving Heavenly Father's delight to give you.

Jesse Duplantis in his book, *Heaven, Close Encounters of the God Kind*, describes being brought to his home prepared for him in heaven. He was awestruck when he saw his home. It had tall ceilings and crown molding, and the furniture was all done in his favorite taste. Some of it was just like what he had in his home. When Jesse cried out in delight, he was told that the Lord knew his tastes and so they put that in his home, all his desires and some he had never thought of. Jesse was delighted.

I had a similar experience. One time when I was praying God showed me a quick peek at my room in heaven. I gasped in delight. It was so me! We lived in a double wide trailer years ago and I loved my bedroom there. It was my favorite bedroom I had ever had. My sister and I decorated it. It had wallpaper that I loved. The wallpaper looked kind of Victorian with long vertical yellow stripes and bouquets of roses along the stripes. The color scheme was yellow, pink and a little blue in the bouquets.

To my delight, my room in heaven was a glorified version of that bedroom. It was a rounded room that was two stories high. It was wallpapered with my wallpaper I loved so much. The bed was huge and was rounded to fit in the rounded walls and had a huge brass headboard. On either side of the bed were floor to ceiling windows that opened onto a terrace with white sheer curtains tied to either side. I literally cried in delight. The best way I could describe it was it was so, so, so, ME! I loved it. The thing that amazes me so much is that usually I don't even know what I like. Yet when I saw this room, I realized how much

I loved every detail. The Lord knows me better than I know myself. That touches me in a way I cannot express.

Getting back to my point, heaven is a place of only good. I have only touched on one tiny point in heaven but there is so much more. Every one of our senses will be delighted there, beautiful smells, wonderful music, delicious foods, beautiful scenery and every kind of comfort is in heaven. All darkness and evil have been removed, there is not a trace.

On the other hand, hell is a place where all good has been removed. It is separation from God. There is no light there, only darkness. There is no love there whatsoever. Not a hint of compassion. Cruelty and torture beyond imagination is there. Demonic beings torture and torment hell's inhabitants in every possible way.

Bill Wiese in his book and videos called, *23 Minutes in Hell*, describes his vision of hell. God gave Bill a 23-minute vision of hell that changed his life forever. He now spends his life warning people of its horrors and imploring them not to go there.

In Bill's vision, he found himself in a prison cell. The first thing he noticed was the heat. It was too hot to be alive and yet he was, because in hell you are already dead. Bill also noticed he could hardly move his body; it took great effort because he was so weak. And the air quality was so poor that he continually gasped for breath. As he gasped for air, he only got noxious fumes that smelled of sulfur. He also felt incredible thirst and he longed for a single drop of water to soothe his desperately parched mouth. And the sounds, the sounds were also hideous, he heard constant anguished screaming from the millions of souls in torment and he smelled rotting flesh.

In Bill's cell were two hideous reptilian creatures with huge claws. They were viciously pacing and filled with rage toward God and muttering blasphemies. One picked Bill up and smashed him against the wall with such a huge force that Bill felt his bones break. The other creature picked up Bill and with his claws ripped Bills flesh off of his body. At this point two more creatures entered the cell, and each took a limb of Bills and pulled off each of his limbs. The pain was excruciating.

Bill's vision continues but I think that you can get the picture of how horrible, pure evil without God can be. If we remove God, we have removed goodness, and we are left with gross darkness. We are left into the hands of Satan and his creatures with no hope of rescue, ever. This is where following darkness leads.

Do you think I am trying to scare you? It scares me! The first time I ever read about hell was a book I read about a woman's vision of hell. I was so scared that I had to get rid of the book. I literally shook with fear, I didn't sleep well for quite a while. As much as it upsets me; hell is a real place, and we need to be sober minded about it. After I read about hell, I took inventory of my life. I don't want to go there! I also do not want anyone else to go there!!

Gross Darkness

Our verses in Isaiah describe this separation of light and darkness beginning on earth. We are beginning to see this in our time. Darkness on earth is growing. It is only going to get worse. As light and darkness are separating and moving away from each other, the light is growing more glorious and the darkness more gross.

Mankind is embracing sin and wickedness at a whole new level. We have seen our whole society embrace murder, {abortion} and sexual immorality, {free sex and homosexuality} and this is just the beginning, evil has no bounds bestiality and sex with evil spirits is just around the corner.

But that is not all; greed has run rampant, greed in huge proportions. Greed is in every aspect of our lives. Almost every business from banks to hospitals and drug companies to food manufacturers are out for one thing, PROFIT. It comes first. Human life is no longer important. That is just a small sample the list continues. Scams are everywhere. Even some in government have become totally corrupt. Politicians do things that would put you and I in prison.

Hatred is growing. Fear is growing. Depression and mental illness are an epidemic. Darkness is increasing and those who are part of that kingdom are progressing deeper and deeper into darkness, gross darkness. This will only continue until it comes to full fruition.

Glorious Light

On the other hand, those who belong to the kingdom of light will begin to shine brighter. This comes from an intimate relationship with Jesus. This comes from obedience and cooperation with the Holy Spirit who is conforming us into the image of Jesus.

There will be no more sitting on the fence in the body of Christ. We will either be on one side or the other, darkness or light. We can no longer be in the middle. Those in the kingdom of light will separate themselves from the sin of this world and walk in holiness, cleansing themselves and drawing closer to God. We will truly become the light of the world. The light that brings chaos into order, the light that leads others out of darkness and the kind of light that torments darkness.

John Paul Jackson's Vision

John Paul Jackson, the prophet, {who I especially like because he helped me at a desperate time in my life,} had a vision of a young Christian girl. This young girl had to move out of her apartment and into another apartment that wasn't quite as nice. John Paul saw in the spirit what was going on to this young girl and to the spiritual realm around her.

She was not happy about the move, but the move was God's plan, because as she moved into the new apartment building her presence changed everything. The light within her changed the whole atmosphere of the apartment building. John saw the demonic spirits that had ruled in the apartment building scream in torment as she moved in. God had planned her presence there for that very reason.

They shrieked, "The light has come, the light has come!!" And they fled from the building.

This young Christian was oblivious to what her presence was doing around her. She was unaware of the powerful effect that the light of Christ within her was having.

Then John saw her head to the store for some groceries. She wanted to go to a closer store but because of traffic she was not able to make the lane change in time and proceeded down the road to the next store. She seemed irritated and upset. She hadn't wanted to move, and everything seemed to be going wrong, now this. After she filled her cart and headed to the checkout someone pushed ahead of her, which irritated her again and she headed to another line.

What John was shown in the vision and yet the young girl did not know, was that this all was part of God's plan. God wanted her at that particular store with that particular cashier. The light coming from this young Christian girl was needed to minister to this cashier.

God sent enough Christians through this cashier's line, that the light coming from them was able to break the darkness around her and she would come to the Lord.

The light coming from this young Christian was shining to those around her and though she did not realize it. She was where she needed to be. She was having a profound effect everywhere she went. Everything that she was going through was planned for a reason, God was using her!

The light in us is God's light. This light will change everything! It breaks up the darkness around us!

In the Image of God

We were created in God's image.

Then God said, "Let Us make man in Our image, according to our likeness; let them have dominion over the fish of the sea, over the birds of the air, and over the cattle, over all the earth and over every creeping thing that creeps on the earth." So, God created man in His own image: in the image of God, He created him; male and female He created them. Genesis 1:26-27

God has made us like Him. Adam sinned and fell and so did all mankind, but Christ became the second Adam and redeemed us. We who choose to follow Christ and become born again we have a deposit of Christ within us. He has placed His light within us. The same light, the same frequency, the same thing! This is in our spirit man, not our souls. {Our soul is still unregenerate and has to be worked on.}

We are to be the light of the world. God has placed His light in us, and we are to rule and reign here as he commanded Adam to do. So, what are we to do? How do we do this?

Isaiah 60:1 says, *Arise, shine;* This is a commandment. We are to do it.

Matthew 5:14-16, says You are the light of the world. A city set on a hill cannot be hidden. Nor do they light a lamp and put it under a basket, but on a lampstand and it gives light to all who are in the house. Let your light so shine before men, that they may see your good works and glorify your Father in heaven. This also sounds like it is our part to do.

Ephesians 5:8-11 says, for you were once darkness, but now you are light in the Lord. Walk as children of the light [for the fruit of the spirit is in all goodness righteousness and truth], finding out what is acceptable to the Lord. And have no fellowship with the unfruitful works of darkness, but rather expose them. This is also telling us to walk in light and stay away from darkness. It is up to us.

Romans 13:12-14 says, The night is far spent, the day is at hand. Therefore, let us cast off the works of darkness, and let us put on the armor of light. Let us walk properly, as in the day, not in revelry and drunkenness, not in lewdness and lust, not in strife and envy. But put on the Lord Jesus Christ and make no provision for the flesh, to fulfill its lusts. We are to cast of darkness and put on Christ. This is again up to us.

We have a responsibility to walk in the light and to stay away from darkness. We are the light of the world. We have to cast off darkness. We can no longer live in light and darkness. These two are separating. Light will become brighter and brighter as darkness is separated and only what is pure and good remains. The darkness is heading the opposite direction and soon those who walk that way will become completely dark. We can no longer hide our light under a bushel because as we shine many will leave the darkness and turn to the light.

Chapter Nineteen

Letting Light into our Dark Places

Living in the light means continuing to get closer to God and letting His light into all those dark places that are still in my soul. Coming to the light can also be painful at times. Light shines up all that is within us and that is truly painful. Darkness hides our sin, our hurts, pain and fears. Darkness keeps us wrapped up in all the lies we chose to believe. The light exposes all that is in me that is dark and ugly. There are some horrible things inside of me and they are very hard to face. The light will expose them.

One of those things was fear. Fear ruled my entire life and had to be dealt with. I was afraid of seemingly everything and everybody. I was like a child inside even though I was an adult on the outside. I felt small and afraid of everything. But certain things especially terrified me.

The worst things were nighttime and the dark, men and being alone with men and worst of all smelling alcohol on someone's breath. These things put me into irrational terror. Dealing with it took many years but it began with dealing with my worst nightmare, a literal nightmare.

As long as I can remember I had the same dream, over and over. The dream held such terror for me that I was actually afraid of dreaming; I dreaded dreams. The dream, itself doesn't sound all that scary but the feeling behind it was and I would wake up shaking in terror. In the dream, I am always looking through a closet; I am fine until all of a sudden, I notice at the back of the closet is a small door. The minute I see the door I feel such terror that it is hard to describe such terror. I know there is something so horrible behind that little door that I wake up shaking and crying. The dream terrified me my whole childhood and even as an adult.

I just passed it off as "just a dream" until I was in my early twenties and God started dealing with me that dreams are messages from Him. I realized there was something I was missing. God was telling me something. This was real.

One afternoon, when I was in my early twenties I decided to deal with my nightmare. So, I waited until I had my children in bed for their nap, {I had a two-year-old and a four-year-old} and I decided to pray about it. I got into a place of prayer, and I went to the back of that closet, the one from my dream, and I opened the little door at the back of that closet.

Suddenly I was no longer in my twenties; I was

transported to another time and place, deep in my past. I was in my crib, and I was about two years old in a dark bedroom. I didn't know a memory could be so real. I was there and I was two again, I was thinking and feeling like a two-year-old. There was a figure looming over my crib. He looked larger than life because of my small size and he was very terrifying. I knew he was going to hurt me. It was a man, an evil man, my stepfather. The fear I felt was greater than any fear I have ever felt before.

I immediately opened my eyes, I had to come out of that place, the terror was greater than I could handle. I ran to the bedroom for my children for comfort. I needed someone. I fell on my bed shaking and trembling in fear and woke up my children from their naps because I was so scared that I needed them. It was no wonder I was living in fear because of the terror that was locked in darkness inside of me.

I could not bear to open that door again on my own, but God prepared a day and time with the help of a Christian counselor and that door was opened again. Behind that door was horror and pain and much darkness.

But opening that door allowed me healing and deliverance. God's light went into the dark places of my soul and brought healing.

It is okay to feel pain. Pain is a bridge to healing. Allow yourself to feel your pain and bring your pain to Jesus. I have used pain and tears as a prayer, more times than I could count. I lift my heart as it is to the Lord, pain and tears and all. Continually bringing our pain to Jesus will protect us from the enemy getting a foothold or a dark place in our heart. Burying our pain can be dangerous.

We all have dark places hiding inside us that we need to bring to the light of the Lord. Satan wants to keep these places in us because through them he has control over us. He had complete control over me for years through fear. He kept me in constant torment.

Satan will seek, through some kind of trauma or difficult life situation, to fragment our soul and he holds that part of us as a prisoner in darkness. As we begin to turn these dark areas within us over to the light of the Lord we begin to walk in freedom.

This is what happened to me as a small two-year-old child with a pedophile stepfather. But as God's light began to take over this area, I was finally able to grow up on the inside and no longer live life cowering and hiding.

This is not something you have to do yourself. The Holy Spirit's work within us will bring to light the dark areas of our souls. We need to simply ask Him and cooperate with Him as He reveals the problem areas and painful memories. Our best Friend lives inside of us and we are not alone even in our own skin.

This was only one area in my life that God dealt with, there were many more to come. The process has taken years, but God is very patient and delicate with us, we are precious to Him and He handles us gently.

We also inherit darkness from our ancestors. Curses are passed down from our family line. In my family line night terrors and asthma were passed down, in my husband's family alcoholism and mental illness. These are areas of darkness that need to be retaken from the enemy in our family lines. This can be done by repenting for the sins of our forefathers and coming under the blood of Jesus.

The sacrifice of Jesus is the trump card in the spirit realm. It will cover every sin of our own and our family line. Repentance and faith in His blood activates the work of the blood of Jesus in our lives. Humility and fear of the Lord activates true repentance. There is no place for pride in our lives, at least not mine. I am too big of a mess.

I read something really good one time. It compared our soul to a house. Each room in the house was compared to a compartment of our soul. The living room, kitchen, bathroom, bedrooms, closets, etc. Each stood for an aspect of our personality. Some of the rooms had been cleaned and were full of light. These rooms had been turned over to the Lord. Other rooms had the curtains drawn and were dark dusty and full of garbage. These rooms were areas not turned over to Him.

I used this illustration in prayer. Walking through the rooms of my soul and opening doors. Then inviting Jesus into every area and corner to chase away the darkness and the cobwebs and bring His light. This has to be done so that we can let our light shine, the true light. The light of the Lord Jesus living inside of us. Our part is living in humble and loving submission to Him. He offers us freedom and not being controlled by darkness or evil but living in a heart filled with light.

Chapter Twenty
The Switch

The thief does not come except to steal, and to kill, and to destroy. I have come that they may have life, and that they may have it more abundantly. John 10:10

Light glorious light, we are called to this. God has translated us out of the kingdom of darkness and now we are light. We have within us the light of God. It has the same frequency it has the same substance as Jesus. The same power that raised Jesus Christ from the dead is working in us. What a glorious thought!

Light is energy and power. God is a being of light and love. Both are incredible forces that defeat all hate and darkness. Both of these forces are life to us. We are created in God's image. We were meant to be beings of light.

I believe there is a link between light and love. I

believe love appears as light. In God's immediate presence the light is indescribable. He is so bright and the power around His throne is immense that witnesses to the throne of God are amazed at the sight and usually become weak and unable to stand or even lift their heads.

I want to quote one little sentence from someone who has visited God's throne and seen God in His brightness. This comes from the book, *The Throne Room Company,* by Shawn Bolz. He says: **In the center of the room was the glorified Son. His presence was so bright that the pure light coming from His face felt like a walk into the heart of a nuclear explosion. Yet somehow, He gave me the grace to walk toward Him.**

God is actually most likely much brighter than a nuclear explosion. God is light and He created light to form the universe with. Only a small spectrum of this light is visible to us. Physical light enables our bodies to live just as spiritual light is essential to our spirit being.

We have learned that how we live either attracts light or darkness. Our deeds, thoughts, actions, emotions and words are seen in the spirit realm. They also have color, aroma and taste. We are either clothing ourselves in light or darkness by how we live. The closer we walk with the Lord and the more we saturate ourselves with His presence the more light we will have within us. The more light we have within us the more we will repel the darkness.

Darkness and the End of the Age

We, on earth, are rapidly coming to the end of this age. Darkness is getting darker, and light is getting brighter. We are called to be the light of the earth at this time. We are to leave the worldly system set up by Satan at the beginning of the age by Nimrod. That is the kingdom of darkness that walks in rebellion to God. It is prideful and humanistic and seeks fulfillment apart from God. It is signified by Babylon. It is the spirit of the world and the worldly way of thinking. That kingdom will have its ultimate show down with the God's kingdom in the Battle of Armageddon. They will literally declare war on God. They will come to a quick ending. They will suffer eternal torment.

We are to come out of darkness and walk in the light, and rise and shine, and have no part of the darkness. These are commandments. Because God will soon separate the light and darkness forever, all good and all evil will be separated for all eternity. Each of us will go one way or another, permanently.

Switching Kingdoms,

I used to belong in the kingdom of darkness. It was a constant downward spiral. I had no peace, no love, no joy and no light. My actions hurt myself and others. From the time I woke up in the morning until I went to bed at night, I continually tried to fill the emptiness inside me. The emptiness only seemed to get bigger.

I could sense the difference in those who belonged to the kingdom of light. They repelled me. They seemed so clean, "so goody two shoes." I would cuss when they spoke of the Lord. I didn't like to hear about it. It angered me. It threatened me.

I was wrapped up in darkness and it showed. It showed in the words I spoke and the way I dressed, in the music I listened to and the friends I chose. It showed in the way I treated myself and others. I was on a path of destruction. I thought I was free, but I wasn't, I was trapped. When I finally realized I was trapped I thought it was too late.

It was at this point Jesus walked into the room I was in and told me He loved me. In that instant, I switched kingdoms. I was transformed on the inside. The Light was so beautiful I instantly cried out, "I want God!"

I now despised darkness. I embraced Jesus with everything I had. I was drowning and His hand lifted me out and rescued me.

The change was immediate, and the change was profound. I felt peace and joy instead of constant torment. I loved the light, and I was filled with it. I was free from the bad habits that bound me. Everything changed from that moment on because I wanted nothing more to do with darkness. The records I listened to went in the trash. I stopped seeing my old friends, my speech changed, my clothes and the way I spent my time. But even more than that, the inside of me changed. I now had a relationship with God. He was real to me now and He was with me all the time. I was loved and I belonged to him.

A couple of times, soon after this, I woke up in the morning to the same old depression, and then suddenly I would remember, "I belong to Jesus, now." And the depression would immediately fade, and the peace would return. The relief I felt coming out of darkness was profound.

I walked around in awe. I had never noticed the world before, the blue sky, the flowers and the trees. I was in the same world, but it seemed like a whole new place. I had truly switched kingdoms. I couldn't even litter anymore. I loved Light, now!!!!

Flipping the Switch

Remember my story in the introduction of this book, of my waking up in pitch blackness. My terror of waking up disoriented and afraid in a pitch-dark room ended as soon as I flipped on the light switch. The darkness had so disoriented me that I was afraid I was in hell. My mind was convinced evil beings were surrounding me and I was about to be devoured.

But the darkness disappeared in a fraction of a second, when the light came. The evil, the fear and the confusion disappeared. It was replaced with comfort; relief and I was sure now where I was. All I had to do is flip the switch.

Light is stronger than darkness. Light chases away the darkness. Darkness is void and empty. Light is power and energy.

The earth lies in the power of the evil one. He has set up a kingdom of darkness on this planet and its effects can be seen everywhere, anywhere that there is pain and suffering. Satan seeks three things to kill to steal and to destroy. That is the work of darkness.

Jesus told us He is the Light of the world, and He has come to give us life and life more abundantly. The work of light is complete restoration.

Jesus is our answer. He is our light switch. His light brings chaos back into order again. He breaks the power of evil and darkness that holds us. In every area that holds darkness in our lives, we need to flip on the light switch and turn on the light of Jesus and dispel the darkness.

There are two kingdoms reigning on this earth. The door to both is here, the entrance to light and the entrance to darkness. The choice is ours and the light switch is available. Go ahead flip the switch, turn on the LIGHT! Jesus!

Epilogue

I wanted to be sure that you, my reader, have switched kingdoms, that you have been translated out of the kingdom of darkness and into the kingdom of light. The only way to do this is through Jesus and the sacrifice He made for you on the cross.

The longer that I serve the Lord and the more I get to know, the more I realize how personal and how intimately acquainted with you, and I, that God really is. He knows us inside and out. He actually knows you and all about you way more than you even know your own self. And He still loves you, more than you could possibly realize. That is His nature. Love is light, pure light.

Jesus paid a great price for you; He has paid it with His own blood. Would you like to receive this gift of redemption out of the kingdom of darkness?

Let's ask Him now, Lord Jesus, I ask you to be my Lord and Savior, right now I give you myself. I ask you to forgive my sins and receive me into your Kingdom of Light.

Now, take a deep breath. Something very important has just happened, you have switched kingdoms. Something has changed on the inside of you. Your spirit has been reborn. Welcome to the Kingdom of Light.

Notes

Chapter 1....... *Heaven, Close Encounters of the God Kind,* By Jesse Duplantis   Harrison House, Tulsa Oklahoma, pages 113-114

  While Out of My Body I saw God Heaven and the Living Dead, by Dr. Rogelio Mills Trinity Publishing Co. St Clair Shores, Michigan pages 81-82

Paradise, the Holy City and the Glory of the Throne, by Rev. Elwood Scott   Engeltal Press, Jasper ARK pages 142-143

 In Heaven, By Dean Braxton, Xulon Press , page 121

Chapter 4......*Delivered,* by Tamara Laroux

Chapter 5.....*The Blessing*, by Gary Smalley and John Trent

Chapter 6......*Paradise. The Holy City and the Glory of the Throne,* by Rev Elwood Scott
Engeltal Press, Jasper ARK page 146

Chapter 9....... *Becoming Like Jesus part 2,* by Neville Johnson

Paradise the Holy City and the Glory of the Throne, by Elwood Scott
Engeltal Press, Jasper ARK pages 142-143

The Precious Secret, by Fulton Oursler
The John C. Winston Co, Philadelphia-Toronto, pages 138-139

Chapter 10…..*Heaven, Close Encounters of the God Kind,* by
Jesse Duplantis   Harrison House, Tulsa Oklahoma, pages 88-89

The Heavens Opened, by Anna Rountree
Creation House, Lake Mary, Florida page 31

Chapter 20..*The Throne Room Company,* by Shawn Bolz
Streams Publishing House, North Sutton, New Hampshire page
20

www.ingramcontent.com/pod-product-compliance
Lightning Source LLC
LaVergne TN
LVHW011224080426
835509LV00005B/313